Mathematics
(Intermediate Tier)

Linda Newlands
Sally Russell
Ron Joyner

Walrus Books Ltd

National Curriculum, Key Stage 4   **Mathematics**   Intermediate Tier

Section	Page number
Introduction	1
Number	
Numbers	2
Rounding	6
Approximation	7
Properties of numbers	9
Percentages	16
Ratio	20
Rates	23
Time	27
Exponential decay	29
Algebra	
Sequences	30
Formulae & equations	32
Reciprocals	34
Flow charts	34
Solving equations	35
Algebraic manipulation	36
Brackets	40
Graphs	42
Rates	47
Proportionality	49
Inequalities	50

Section	Page number
Shape and Space	
Three dimensional objects & their representation	54
Linear measurements	55
Angles	57
Bearings	60
Plane shapes	61
Similar shapes	62
Circles	63
Loci	66
Construction	67
Measures	68
Pythagoras	69
Areas	70
Enlargement & reduction	73
Symmetries	75
Vectors	79
Trigonometry	83
Identifying formulae	85
Handling Data	
Statistics	88
Presenting data	90
Frequency diagrams	92
Averages and spreads	95
Interpreting data	100
Probability	102
Combinations of events	106
Tree diagrams	108
Questions	109
Answers	118
Index	124

© Linda Newlands, Sally Russell, & Ron Joyner 1994, 1998.
All rights are reserved. No part of this publication (illustrations or text) may be reproduced without prior permission of the authors.

First printed: January 1994
Revised and reprinted: October 1994
Reprinted with corrections : September 1995
Completely revised : January 1998

ISBN 1-900290-15-4

Information about this guide and how to get the best from it.

This booklet is a revision guide so all the points are set out as briefly as possible. It contains the topics you will need to know for any examination syllabus which targets up to Grade B.

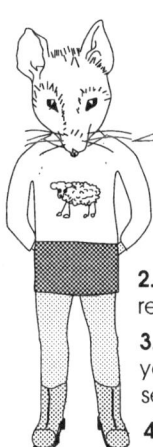

As everyone knows, good advice is easy to give, but often it is so hard to follow. Do give some of the ideas on this page a try.

1. Ask your teacher to explain the bits that you don't understand, or bits which seem to be wrong. (Even with careful checking, **mistakes do get through**.)

2. The sad truth is that you will have to work hard during revision, just reading the guide will not do the trick.

3. Whenever possible, use a pencil and paper. Get your text book and revision guide open at the same section and compare the two treatments.

4. Start each work session by going back over the last section you covered. A quick reminder before the information fades tends to make it stick much longer.

5. Rather than working for a set time, decide on which section you want to get done and then keep going until you feel comfortable with the contents.

Very Important: The animals are not included because I want to patronise the reader. They are there to break up the blocks of text. Usually, what they say is relevant to that bit of mathematics. I choose animals rather than people because I find them easier to draw.

I have set out my work space the way I like it: plenty of paper, some pens, my glass of fizzy water and the guide open with only the margin visible.

That way I can test myself by only uncovering the right hand side when I have tried to remember the details.

These three pictures (icons) are used as a shorthand.

paper covering the information

keywords are visible

This icon accompanies the key strokes needed on a calculator.

This icon appears in the margin whenever there is an example nearby.

Tarsiers live in the forests of Sumatra, Borneo, Java, the Philippines and the Celebese Islands. They are nocturnal insectivores; the one used in the guide indicates an answer.

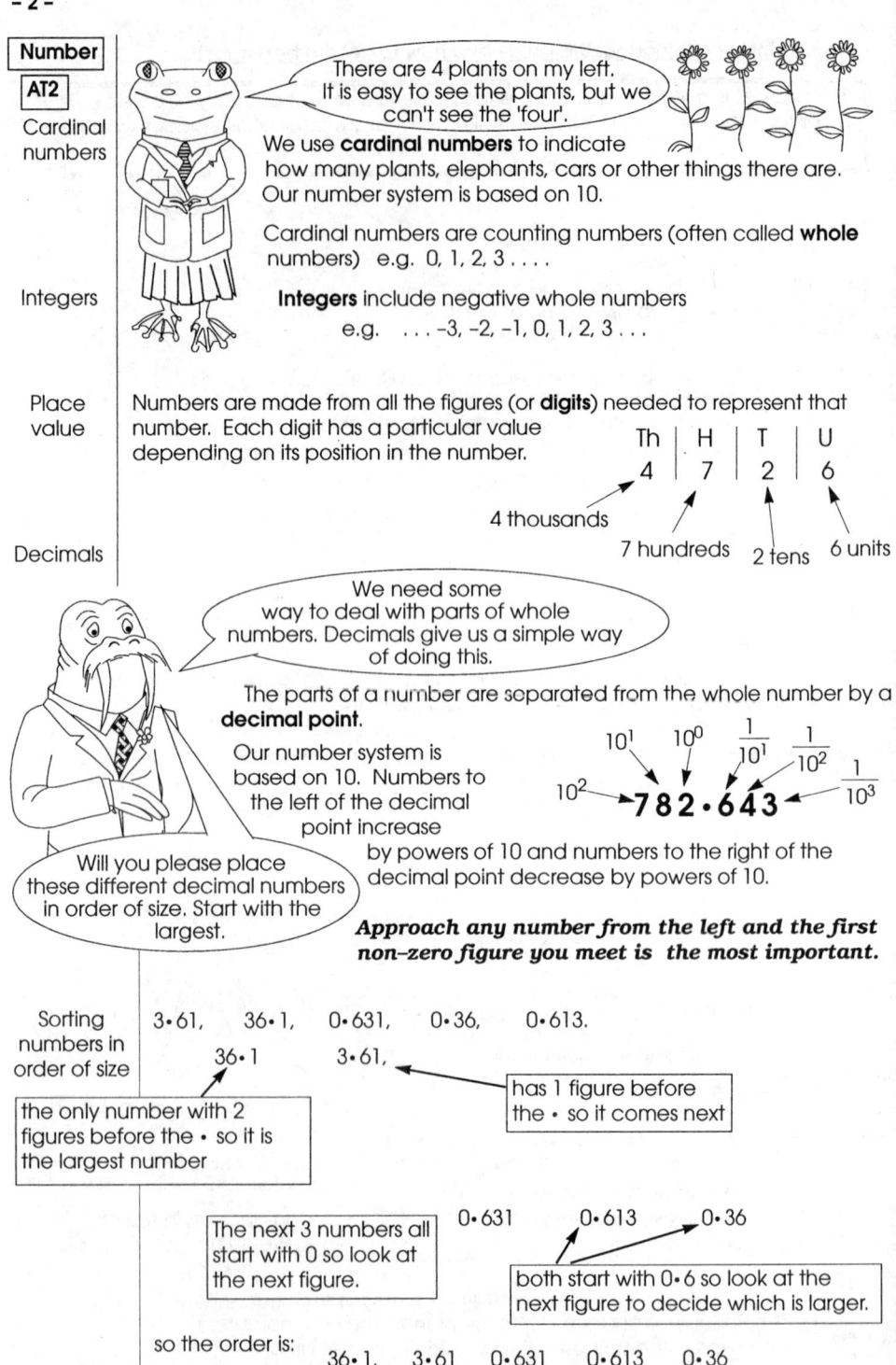

Number

AT2

Cardinal numbers

> There are 4 plants on my left. It is easy to see the plants, but we can't see the 'four'.

We use **cardinal numbers** to indicate how many plants, elephants, cars or other things there are. Our number system is based on 10.

Cardinal numbers are counting numbers (often called **whole numbers**) e.g. 0, 1, 2, 3 . . . .

Integers

Integers include negative whole numbers
e.g. . . . –3, –2, –1, 0, 1, 2, 3 . . .

Place value

Numbers are made from all the figures (or **digits**) needed to represent that number. Each digit has a particular value depending on its position in the number.

Th	H	T	U
4	7	2	6

4 thousands
7 hundreds
2 tens
6 units

Decimals

> We need some way to deal with parts of whole numbers. Decimals give us a simple way of doing this.

The parts of a number are separated from the whole number by a **decimal point**.

Our number system is based on 10. Numbers to the left of the decimal point increase by powers of 10 and numbers to the right of the decimal point decrease by powers of 10.

10^2 10^1 10^0 $\frac{1}{10^1}$ $\frac{1}{10^2}$ $\frac{1}{10^3}$

7 8 2 • 6 4 3

> Will you please place these different decimal numbers in order of size. Start with the largest.

Approach any number from the left and the first non-zero figure you meet is the most important.

Sorting numbers in order of size

3•61,   36•1,   0•631,   0•36,   0•613.

36•1 — the only number with 2 figures before the • so it is the largest number

3•61, — has 1 figure before the • so it comes next

The next 3 numbers all start with 0 so look at the next figure.

0•631   0•613   0•36

0•613 and 0•36 — both start with 0•6 so look at the next figure to decide which is larger.

so the order is: 36•1,   3•61,   0•631,   0•613,   0•36

Operations	Calculations are made by doing **operations** on these numbers.

Operations are shown by signs such as: +, −, ×, ÷, etc.

add ⎫
sum ⎬ +
total ⎭

take away ⎫
subtract ⎬ −
difference ⎭

multiply ⎫
times ⎬ ×
of ⎪
product ⎭

divide ⎫
share out of ⎬ ÷
find a ⎪
fraction of ⎭

A 'sum' like 3 + 4 = 7 is easy. You read the sum from left to right, just like reading a book.
The + and × operations give the same answer when the numbers are swapped round.

Commutative operations	2 × 7 = 14 and 7 × 2 = 14
	3 + 5 = 8 and 5 + 3 = 8

+ and × are said to be commutative

− and ÷ are not commutative and so with these two operations, the order in which you deal with the numbers is very important.

e.g. 10 − 8 = 2
8 − 10 does not equal 2
(If you have 8 sweets you cannot eat 10 !)

Read the question carefully and decide whether you can do it in your head or not.

In the head	30 × 400 can be done in your head.

30 × 400 = 12 000
= 3 × 10 × 4 × 100
= 3 × 4 × 10 × 100
= 12 × 1000
= 12 000

Harder questions	147 × 36 This one needs to be done on paper using long multiplication or (if allowed) using your calculator.

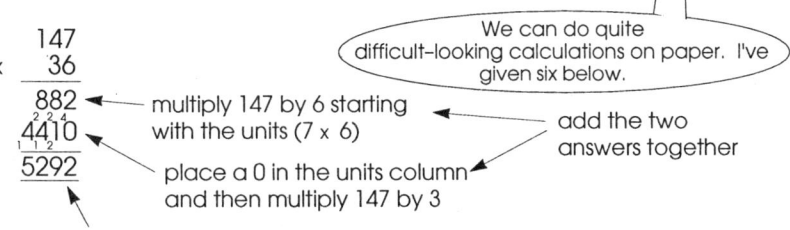

🥚1

```
      147
   ×   36
   ─────
      882  ◄── multiply 147 by 6 starting
     4410       with the units (7 × 6)
   ─────   ◄── add the two
     5292       answers together
              place a 0 in the units column
              and then multiply 147 by 3
```

We can do quite difficult-looking calculations on paper. I've given six below.

You can check your answer is correct by using your calculator.

You may think of an easier way to calculate an answer
e.g. 239 × 99
Work out 239 × 100 and subtract 239 from the answer.

23900 − 239 = 23661

```
   23900
 −   239
  ──────
   23661
```

Number | **AT2**

2.
$$70 \times 37.24$$
$$= 10 \times 7 \times 37.24$$
$$= 10 \times 260.68$$
$$= 2606.8$$

so $70 \times 37.24 = 2606.8$

($70 = 7 \times 10$)

Multiply a decimal by 10 by moving the digits one place to the left.

3.
$$400 \times 0.571$$
$$= 100 \times 4 \times 0.571$$
$$= 100 \times 2.284$$
$$= 228.4$$

so $400 \times 0.571 = 228.4$

($400 = 4 \times 100$)

Multiplying by a number smaller than 1 has a decreasing effect.

4.
Dividing is very similar:

$81.4 \div 0.2$ is the same as $814 \div 2$

Dividing by a number smaller than 1 has an increasing effect.

Multiply by 10 - so the number becomes a whole number,

Multiply the other number by 10.

so $81.4 \div 0.2 = 814 \div 2 = 407$

5.
$$0.411 \div 0.03 = 41.1 \div 3 = 13.7$$

so $0.411 \div 0.03 = 13.7$

Multiply by 100 so 0.03 becomes 3

6.
$425 \div 16$

```
     26 r9
16 )4 2¹⁰5
```

or

```
     26 r9
16 )425
    -32
    105
    -96
      9
```

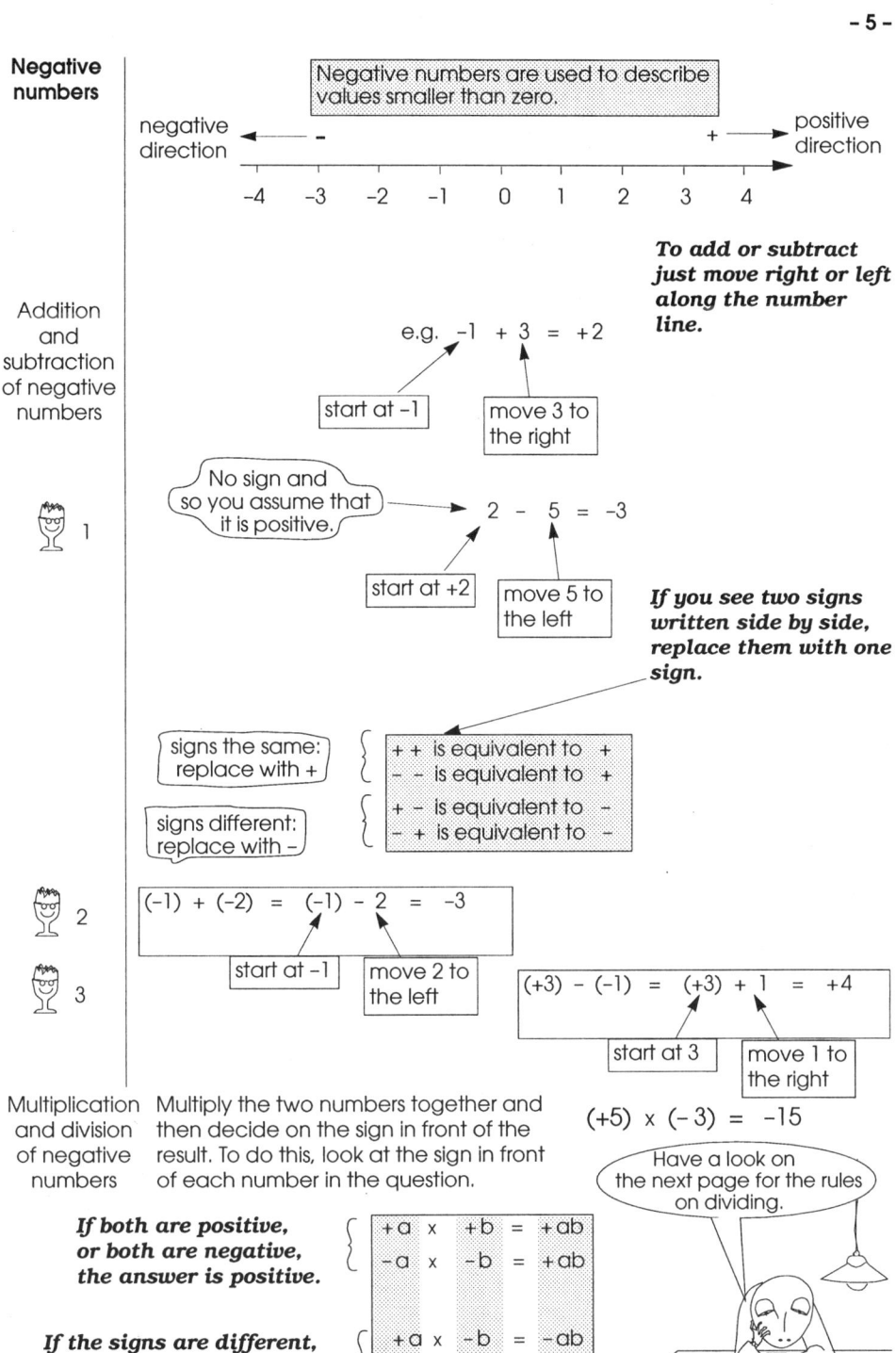

Negative numbers

Negative numbers are used to describe values smaller than zero.

negative direction ← —   + → positive direction

-4 -3 -2 -1 0 1 2 3 4

To add or subtract just move right or left along the number line.

Addition and subtraction of negative numbers

e.g. $-1 + 3 = +2$

- start at -1
- move 3 to the right

😠 1

No sign and so you assume that it is positive.

$2 - 5 = -3$

- start at +2
- move 5 to the left

If you see two signs written side by side, replace them with one sign.

signs the same: replace with +
- $+\,+$ is equivalent to $+$
- $-\,-$ is equivalent to $+$

signs different: replace with −
- $+\,-$ is equivalent to $-$
- $-\,+$ is equivalent to $-$

😠 2 $(-1) + (-2) = (-1) - 2 = -3$

- start at -1
- move 2 to the left

😠 3 $(+3) - (-1) = (+3) + 1 = +4$

- start at 3
- move 1 to the right

Multiplication and division of negative numbers

Multiply the two numbers together and then decide on the sign in front of the result. To do this, look at the sign in front of each number in the question.

$(+5) \times (-3) = -15$

Have a look on the next page for the rules on dividing.

If both are positive, or both are negative, the answer is positive.

- $+a \times +b = +ab$
- $-a \times -b = +ab$

If the signs are different, the answer is negative.

- $+a \times -b = -ab$
- $-a \times +b = -ab$

Number | AT 2

The rules on dividing

If both are positive, or both are negative, the answer is positive.

$$+a \div +b = +\frac{a}{b}$$
$$-a \div -b = +\frac{a}{b}$$

If the signs are different, the answer is negative.

$$+a \div -b = -\frac{a}{b}$$
$$-a \div +b = -\frac{a}{b}$$

$(-15) \div (+5) = -3$
$(-12) \div (-3) = +4$

You might be asked to substitute values into an expression or formula. These values could include negative numbers.

Calculate the value of y in $y = mx + c$
when $m = -2$
      $x = 3$
      $c = -1$

$y = mx + c$
$= (-2)(3) + (-1)$
$= -6 + -1$
$= -7$

Substitute the numbers <u>before</u> trying to calculate an answer. Brackets can help!

N.B. Your calculator might help with these calculations:-
see if it has the $^+/_-$ key.

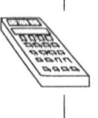

$\boxed{2}\ \boxed{^+/_-}\ \boxed{\times}\ \boxed{3}\ \boxed{=}\ \boxed{+}\ \boxed{1}\ \boxed{^+/_-}\ \boxed{=}\ \boxed{-7}$

Just to be on the safe side

Rounding

Usually numbers have to be written exactly that is, accurately.

But in practical situations, an approximate value may be quite accurate enough.

Pure numbers (not involving measurement) tend to be accurate.

In every day life we usually round off the number to give a workable value, e.g. money is rounded to the nearest penny.

Correcting decimals Find out (usually from the question) how accurate the answer should be.

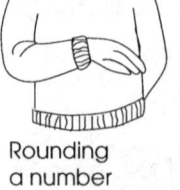

Rounding a number

39 000 at the Big Match

Numbers, particularly large ones, tend to be rounded to give us something that is easy to take in at a glance.

Although the crowd was actually 38 752, 39 000 is quite close enough for it not to be misleading.

(continued on the next page)

– 7 –

| Rounding a number (continued) | The number 38 752 could be rounded to the nearest ten, hundred, thousand – whatever is most convenient. |

to the nearest 10   is   38 750
to the nearest 100   is   38 800
to the nearest 1000   is   39 000

| Rounding remainders | Some problems give an answer with a remainder. You may have to decide if it is sensible to round up or down. In this situation you just have to use your common sense. |

1 Emma has £5.00.
How many ice creams at 65p each can she buy?

$500 \div 65 = 7 \cdot 6923$

This number is nearer 8 than 7 but the ice cream seller will give 7 ice creams and some change.

2 Michael calculates that he will need 4·2 litres of paint for redecorating his bedroom. This rounds to 4 as the nearest whole number but 4 litres would not cover all of the walls – so he must buy 5 litres.

| Decimal places | $3 \cdot 9134 = 3 \cdot 91$ to 2 d.p.
$12 \cdot 25948 = 12 \cdot 26$ to 2 d.p.
$1 \cdot 3981 = 1 \cdot 40$ to 2 d.p. | ***Look at the next figure after that, if it is less than 5 forget it! If it is 5 or more then increase the previous figure by 1.*** |

| Significant figures | Approaching any number from the left, the first non-zero figure is always the most significant (it is the one with the highest place value). |

Round off 574 219 to:
  1 significant figure   = 600 000
  3 significant figures = 574 000
  5 significant figures = 574 220

Remember numbers with 'trapped' zeros e.g. 10 327 has 5 sig. fig.

Round off 0·000 349 48 to:
  1 significant figure   = 0·000 3
  2 significant figures = 0·000 35
  4 significant figures = 0·000 349 5

Approximations Do check that your answers make sense before you write them down. It is all too easy to punch numbers into the calculator and just blindly accept the answer it gives.

1 ***Numbers are usually rounded to 1 significant figure.***

e.g.   372 × 48

round this to the nearest hundred   *round this to the nearest ten*

The answer given by the calculator is 17 856 which is very close to our approximation and so we can write it down with confidence.

i.e.   400   ×   50   =   20 000

(continued)

Number | **AT2**

Approximations

e.g. 2219 ÷ 3·9

round this to the nearest thousand

round this to the nearest unit

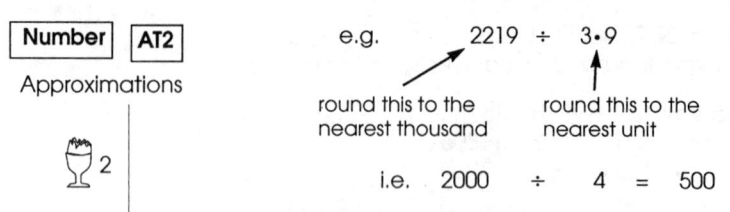

i.e. 2000 ÷ 4 = 500

The answer given by the calculator is 568·97 which is close enough to our approximation.

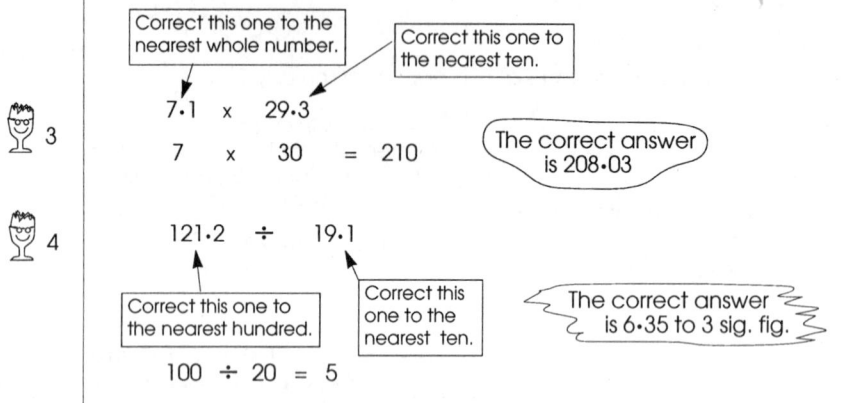

Correct this one to the nearest whole number.

Correct this one to the nearest ten.

7·1 × 29·3

7 × 30 = 210

The correct answer is 208·03

121·2 ÷ 19·1

Correct this one to the nearest hundred.

Correct this one to the nearest ten.

The correct answer is 6·35 to 3 sig. fig.

100 ÷ 20 = 5

Rounding

Always write down the full calculator display **before** rounding to whatever accuracy the exam question specifies.
Never use a rounded figure in a calculation. Use the exact values throughout and correct at the end.

Some problems can only have an approximate solution.
For example if you are asked to find the square root of 27 by using a decimal search you would use a trial and improvement method with your calculator and work to 1 d.p. more than required. Then correct.

Do keep in mind that real-life measurements are almost always approximations. There are two reasons for this.

The object may keep changing e.g. you are taller in the morning than in the evening because your spine compresses slightly through the day. Your weight changes every time you have a drink or go to the loo.

The measuring device can usually be improved to give greater accuracy e.g. the kitchen scales are perfect for cooking but not good enough for the pharmacist.

N.B. When we measure something we try to be as accurate as possible but anyone who sees our measurement knows that it is only accurate to half a unit. If I say that I live 8 kilometres from school people realise that it is unlikely to be exactly 8 km. The real value could be as small as 7·5 km or as large as 8·5 km.

Properties of numbers

Numbers can be given special names just because certain things are true about them...

Definitions of some of these special names are given below.

Even numbers

Even numbers are all the whole numbers that are divisible by 2
(2, 4, 6, 8, 10, ...)

The other counting numbers are **odd**
(1, 3, 5, 7, ...)
(0 is a 'special number')

Prime numbers

Prime numbers are special because they are whole numbers larger than 1 that can **only** be divided by 1 and the number itself e.g. 2, 3, 5, 7, 11, ...37, ... (in other words, a prime number cannot be a multiple of another whole number).

2 is the only even prime.

Numbers can be Very small or very big and can be manipulated into doing all sorts of tricks

Multiples

Multiples are the result of multiplying a number by a positive whole number

e.g. any number multiplied by 3 gives a multiple of 3.
... 3, 6, 9, 12, 15, ...

Factors

Factors of a number are pairs of numbers that multiply together to give the number

e.g. These are the factors of 36:
The factors of 36 are: 1, 2, 3, 4, 6, 9, 12, 18, 36.

```
1 x 36
2 x 18
3 x 12
4 x  9
6 x  6
```

Writing numbers as products of prime numbers Method 1.

All positive numbers can be rewritten as the product (x) of prime numbers.

Keep dividing by the smallest prime number that will divide until you can't, then try the next prime number etc.

```
2 | 36
2 | 18
3 |  9
     3
```
This number is prime so you have finished

Answer: The prime factors of 36 are 2, 2, 3 and 3,
or 36 = $2^2 \times 3^2$

| Number | AT2 |

Method 2.

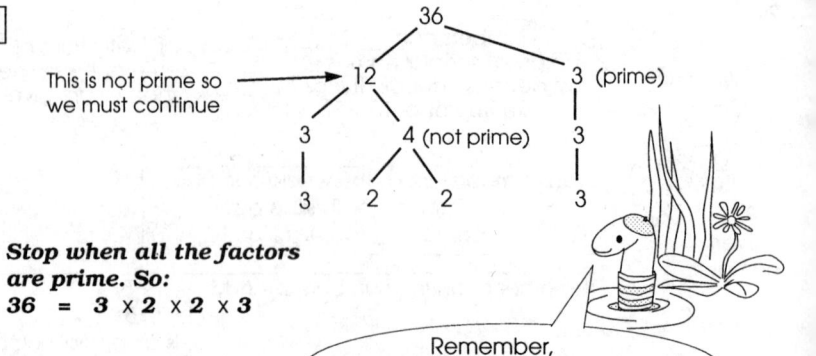

This is not prime so → 12   3 (prime)
we must continue
         3   4 (not prime)   3
         | / \ |
         3 2   2   3

Stop when all the factors are prime. So:
36 = 3 × 2 × 2 × 3

$36 = 2^2 \times 3^2$

Remember, just reading through is not the same as knowing.

Highest common factor

Which numbers (other than 1) divide into both 9 and 36?

These numbers are called factors and the largest number is the highest common factor (HCF).

Factors of 9 = 1, 3, 9
Factors of 36 = 1, 2, 3, 4, 6, 9, 12, 18, 36

The common factors are 1, 3 and 9 - so 9 is the highest common factor.

It helps to write each number in its prime factors :-

e.g. Find the HCF of 84 and 144

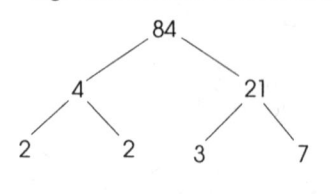

$84 = 2^2 \times 3 \times 7$

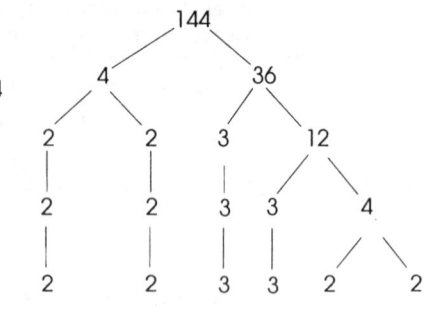

$144 = 2^4 \times 3^2$

Both numbers have factors of 2^2 and 3.
The HCF is $2^2 \times 3$ = 4 × 3 = 12

Lowest common multiple

Sometimes you need to know the smallest number that is a multiple common to 2 or more numbers. This number is called the lowest common multiple.

e.g. Find the lowest common multiple (LCM) of 3, 4 and 18.

Make a list of the first few multiples for each number:

3: 3, 6, 9, 12, 15, 18, 21, 24, 27, 30, 33, 36 - - -
4: 4, 8, 12, 16, 20, 24, 28, 32, 36 - - -
18: 18, 36 - - -

so 36 is the smallest number belonging to all 3 lists.

Finding LCMs is very useful when adding or subtracting fractions.

Squares and square roots

3 × 3 = 9
or 3^2 = 9

square it → 4 → 16
find the square root ←

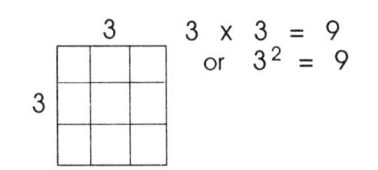

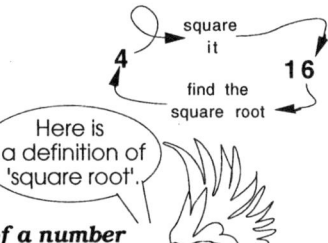

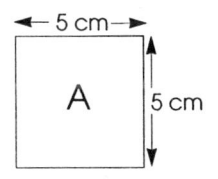

Here is a definition of 'square root'.

The square root of a number will give the number when the square root is multiplied by itself.
If $x \times x = A$
Then $\sqrt{A} = x$

Area of A is 5 cm × 5 cm = 25 cm^2.
25 is called the square of 5
The opposite way of saying this is 5 is the square root of 25.

Square roots on a calculator ($\sqrt{\ }$)

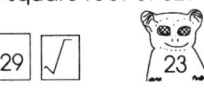

What is the square root of 529 ?

529 √ 23

You will probably not need to use the = button when finding square roots, squares, sin and other functions

Remember that
−23 × −23 = 529
so $\sqrt{529}$ = ±23

another question

What is the hypotenuse of a right angle triangle with the two other sides 5 cm and 3 cm long?

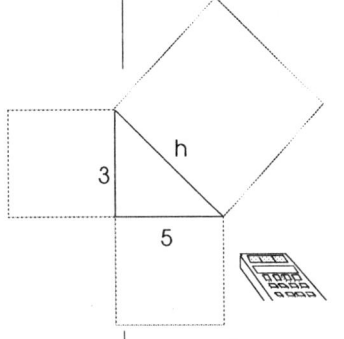

$5^2 + 3^2 = h^2$
$25 + 9 = h^2$
$34 = h^2$

so h must be = $\sqrt{34}$

34 √ 5·83095

The hypotenuse is 5·83 cm

Do remember to correct to 3 significant figures

A triangle cannot have a side with negative length so give only the positive value.

Cubes and cube roots

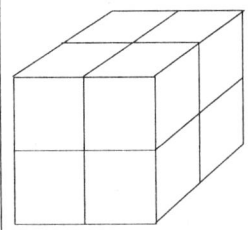

2 × 2 × 2 = 8
or 2^3 = 8

cube it → 2 → 8
find the cube root ←

It is important to note that:

$(-2) \times (-2) \times (-2) = (-2)^3 = -8$

(continued)

- 11 -

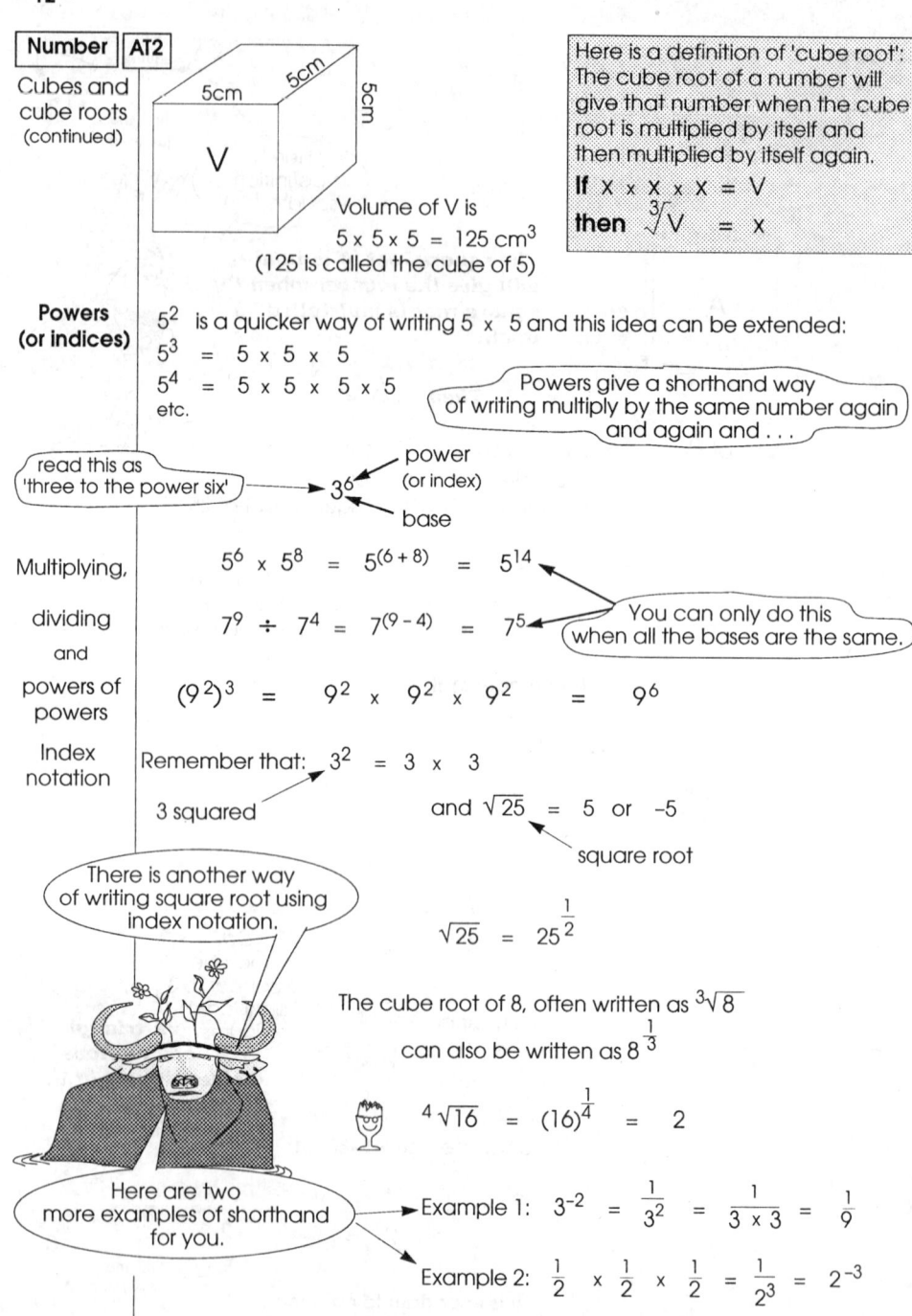

Number | AT2
Cubes and cube roots (continued)

Volume of V is
$5 \times 5 \times 5 = 125 \text{ cm}^3$
(125 is called the cube of 5)

> Here is a definition of 'cube root': The cube root of a number will give that number when the cube root is multiplied by itself and then multiplied by itself again.
> If $x \times x \times x = V$
> then $\sqrt[3]{V} = x$

Powers (or indices)

5^2 is a quicker way of writing 5×5 and this idea can be extended:
$5^3 = 5 \times 5 \times 5$
$5^4 = 5 \times 5 \times 5 \times 5$
etc.

> Powers give a shorthand way of writing multiply by the same number again and again and ...

> read this as 'three to the power six'

3^6 ← power (or index)
  ↖ base

Multiplying, dividing and powers of powers

$5^6 \times 5^8 = 5^{(6+8)} = 5^{14}$

$7^9 \div 7^4 = 7^{(9-4)} = 7^5$

> You can only do this when all the bases are the same.

$(9^2)^3 = 9^2 \times 9^2 \times 9^2 = 9^6$

Index notation

Remember that: $3^2 = 3 \times 3$
  ↑ 3 squared

and $\sqrt{25} = 5$ or -5
  ↑ square root

> There is another way of writing square root using index notation.

$\sqrt{25} = 25^{\frac{1}{2}}$

The cube root of 8, often written as $\sqrt[3]{8}$ can also be written as $8^{\frac{1}{3}}$

$\sqrt[4]{16} = (16)^{\frac{1}{4}} = 2$

> Here are two more examples of shorthand for you.

Example 1: $3^{-2} = \frac{1}{3^2} = \frac{1}{3 \times 3} = \frac{1}{9}$

Example 2: $\frac{1}{2} \times \frac{1}{2} \times \frac{1}{2} = \frac{1}{2^3} = 2^{-3}$

Reciprocal

$3^2 = 3 \times 3 = 9$

$3^{-2} = \dfrac{1}{3^2} = \dfrac{1}{9}$

> The reciprocal of n is $\dfrac{1}{n}$

The reciprocal of 9 is $\dfrac{1}{9}$

or $9 \times \dfrac{1}{9} = 1$

So the reciprocal of 3^2 is 3^{-2}

Standard index form (or standard form)

All numbers can be written in standard form – but it is particularly useful for writing very large or very small numbers.

Numbers in standard form are always in two parts.

$4 \cdot 7 \times 10^8$

- a number between 1 and 10 i.e $1 \leq$ number < 10
- always multiplied
- ten to the power of n where n is an integer

N.B.

7 in standard form is 7×10^0
The power of ten is the interesting part – it tells you how many places the decimal point needs to be moved to return to the original number

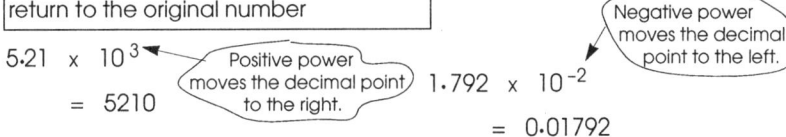

$5 \cdot 21 \times 10^3$
$= 5210$

Positive power moves the decimal point to the right.

$1 \cdot 792 \times 10^{-2}$
$= 0 \cdot 01792$

Negative power moves the decimal point to the left.

Fractions

Some examples of fractions :

$\dfrac{3}{4} \quad \dfrac{1}{103} \quad \dfrac{5}{1}$

$\dfrac{17}{8} \quad \dfrac{15}{25} \quad \dfrac{6}{6}$

$\dfrac{23}{84}$ ← numerator
         ← denominator

Which would you rather have, half of £45 or a quarter of £100 ?

Finding a fraction of a quantity

Here is your question ! Find $^3/_4$ of £125·00.

To do this, we need to divide £125 into 4 equal parts and then find three of these:

| 125 | ÷ | 4 | = | 31·25 |

| 31·25 | × | 3 | = | £93·75 |

(Fractions continue overleaf)

| Number | AT2 |

Equivalent fractions

Try 3 ÷ 4 in your calculator, now try 6 ÷ 8. In each case you will have got the same answer (0·75) because these are equivalent fractions, i.e. they have the same value.

$$\frac{3 \times 2}{4 \times 2} = \frac{6}{8}$$

Reducing to the lowest terms

$^3/_4$ is a fraction which has been reduced to its lowest terms because you cannot divide 3 or 4 by another number to make them into smaller whole numbers.

For example, to reduce $\frac{16}{20}$ to lowest terms we need to find the highest number that will go into 16 and 20, i.e. 4.

$$\frac{16}{20} = \frac{4}{5} \qquad \frac{16 \div 4}{20 \div 4} = \frac{4}{5}$$

Comparing fractions

Your calculator is very useful when comparing fractions because you can express each fraction as a decimal (by dividing the denominator into the numerator)

For example, which is greater, $\frac{4}{7}$ or $\frac{5}{9}$?

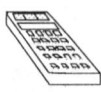

[4] [÷] [7] [=] [0.5714]   [5] [÷] [9] [=] [0.5555]

Ans. $\frac{4}{7}$ is larger than $\frac{5}{9}$

(because 0·5714 is larger than 0·5555)

Did you know . . .

the divide sign and the line in the fraction are the same ?

$$4 \div 7 = \frac{4}{7} \qquad \text{The line means divide by!}$$

Ordering numbers

You may be asked to write some numbers in order:

e.g. Place 0·6, $\frac{5}{8}$, $\frac{6}{11}$, 0·63, $\frac{5}{9}$ in order, writing smallest to largest.

The best way to do this is to convert all the fractions into decimals first, and then write them in order.

$$\frac{5}{8} = 5 \div 8 = 0.625 \qquad \frac{6}{11} = 6 \div 11 = 0.5454$$

$$\frac{5}{9} = 5 \div 9 = 0.5555$$

so the correct order is : $\frac{6}{11}$, $\frac{5}{9}$, 0·6, $\frac{5}{8}$, 0·63

Changing a fraction to a percentage

On page 16 we see how to change a decimal to a percentage. To change a fraction to a percentage you divide the numerator by the denominator and multiply by 100.

Express $\frac{7}{8}$ as a percentage

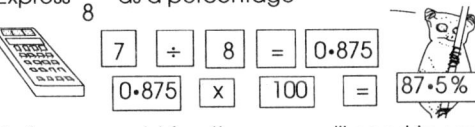

$7 \div 8 = 0.875$
$0.875 \times 100 = 87.5\%$

Adding and subtracting fractions

Before you add fractions, you will need to scale each fraction so that all the denominators are the same. Once that has happened, just add the numerators.

Let's add $\frac{1}{2} + \frac{3}{4} + \frac{3}{8} = \frac{4}{8} + \frac{6}{8} + \frac{3}{8} = \frac{13}{8} = 1\frac{5}{8}$

Mixed fractions are just whole numbers and fractions together. e.g. $2\frac{1}{2}$

Subtracting mixed fractions

e.g. $3\frac{3}{5} - 2\frac{1}{3} = \frac{18}{5} - \frac{7}{3} = \frac{54}{15} - \frac{35}{15} = \frac{19}{15} = 1\frac{4}{15}$

Multiplying fractions

$\frac{2}{3} \times \frac{4}{7} = \frac{8}{21}$ (2×4) — Multiply the numerators
(3×7) — Multiply the denominators

Sometimes a number above the line has a common factor with a number below the line – then you can cancel.

$\frac{\cancel{3}^1}{5} \times \frac{7}{\cancel{12}_4} = \frac{7}{20}$ (1×7)
(5×4)

Mixed numbers have to be turned into improper fractions

e.g. $3\frac{1}{2} \times 1\frac{1}{3} = \frac{7}{\cancel{2}_1} \times \frac{\cancel{4}^2}{3} = \frac{14}{3} = 4\frac{2}{3}$

Dividing fractions is nearly as easy ... change the ÷ to × and turn the second fraction upside down.

Dividing fractions

$\frac{9}{14} \div \frac{3}{5} = \frac{\cancel{9}^3}{14} \times \frac{5}{\cancel{3}_1} = \frac{15}{14} = 1\frac{1}{14}$

(Another half a page on fractions overleaf)

Number

Fractional changes

AT2

Increase 32 by $\frac{3}{4}$ of itself.

Remember that 'of' can be replaced with x.

1. Find $\frac{3}{4} \times \overset{8}{\underset{1}{\cancel{32}}} = 24$ and add it on

   $24 + 32 = 56$

   Or

   $1\frac{3}{4} \times 32 = \frac{7}{\underset{1}{\cancel{4}}} \times \overset{8}{\cancel{32}} = 56$

Decrease 18 by $\frac{1}{3}$ of itself.

2. Find $\frac{1}{3} \times 18 = 6$ and subtract this

   $18 - 6 = 12$

   Or

   Decreasing by $\frac{1}{3}$, leaves $\frac{2}{3}$ $\left(1 - \frac{1}{3} = \frac{2}{3}\right)$

   $\frac{2}{\underset{1}{\cancel{3}}} \times \overset{6}{\cancel{18}} = 12$

Percentages

The VAT inspector, tax collector, shopkeeper and teacher are only a few examples of people who use percentages frequently.

A rat who gets 85 out of 100 marks in an examination has earned 85 per cent and we write this as 85% ;

Per cent just means 'per 100'.

If you have a recurring decimal on your display, round it off to 4 decimal places, or put it all in the memory to use for further calculations.

Percentage as a fraction

To write a percentage as a fraction, just write it as a fraction with denominator of 100.

e.g. 85% as a fraction is $\frac{85}{100}$

Percentage as a decimal

To do this conversion write the percentage as a fraction and then change it to a decimal.

e.g. to get 62% as a decimal

$62\% = \frac{62}{100} = 62 \div 100 = 0.62$

Change a decimal into a percentage by multiplying by 100

e.g. $0.329 \times 100 = 32.9\%$

So $33\% = \frac{33}{100} = 0.33$

Calculating the Percentage of a quantity

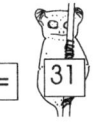

Find 62% of 50 marks.

[0.62] × [50] = [31]   The student got $\frac{31}{50}$

Increasing or decreasing by a given percentage

Shops use percentage increases and decreases to adjust the price of their goods.

Calculating the new price

The old price was £21.00

10% of this is can be calculated as follows:

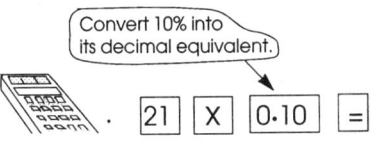

Convert 10% into its decimal equivalent.

[21] × [0.10] = [£2.10]

so you will pay £21 − £2.10 = £18.90

(Or you can just calculate 90% of £21.00 by multiplying by 0.90 : this is a bit faster)

£21.00 × 0.90 = £18.90

your display reads 2.1 but remember, money needs 2 digits after the decimal point.

A mouse wants to increase the length of string on his conker by 15% because he thinks he'll win more games that way. It is currently 45 cm long, so :

[45] × [0.15] = [6.75]

New total is 45 + 6.75 = 51.75 cm

(or calculate directly by

Increase is 15%, so new amount is 115%.

[45] × [1.15] = [51.75])

Expressing one quantity as a % of another

Turtle gets 27 marks out of 45.

It is written on her paper as $\frac{27}{45}$

[27] ÷ [45] = [0.6]

0.6 × 100 = 60%

So Turtle gets 60%

(**Remember, 0.06 would be 6% because percentages are out of 100 and the 2nd decimal place is hundredths**).

Calculate the actual increase :

Our pocket money has been increased from £1.20 a week to £1.80 !

£1.80 − £1.20 = £0.60

and write it as a fraction, comparing it with the original amount

This increase has been written as a percentage.

$\frac{0.60}{1.20}$ = 0.5 = 50%

(0.5 × 100 = 50%)

So they have had a 50% increase in their pocket money.

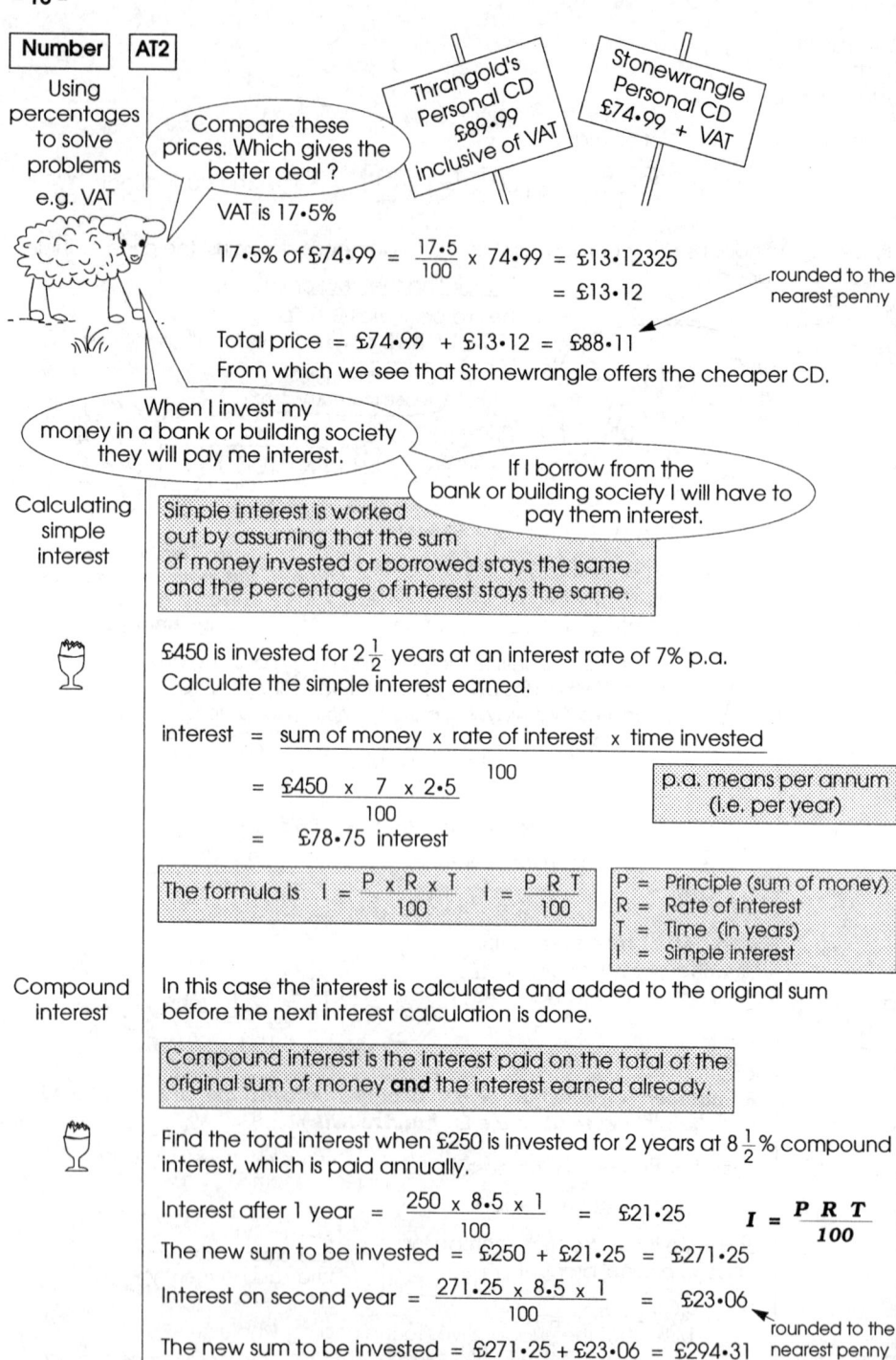

Number — AT2

Using percentages to solve problems
e.g. VAT

Compare these prices. Which gives the better deal?

Thrangold's Personal CD £89·99 inclusive of VAT

Stonewrangle Personal CD £74·99 + VAT

VAT is 17·5%

17·5% of £74·99 = $\frac{17 \cdot 5}{100}$ × 74·99 = £13·12325

= £13·12 ← rounded to the nearest penny

Total price = £74·99 + £13·12 = £88·11

From which we see that Stonewrangle offers the cheaper CD.

When I invest my money in a bank or building society they will pay me interest.

If I borrow from the bank or building society I will have to pay them interest.

Calculating simple interest

Simple interest is worked out by assuming that the sum of money invested or borrowed stays the same and the percentage of interest stays the same.

£450 is invested for $2\frac{1}{2}$ years at an interest rate of 7% p.a. Calculate the simple interest earned.

interest = sum of money × rate of interest × time invested
                                    100

= $\frac{£450 \times 7 \times 2 \cdot 5}{100}$

= £78·75 interest

p.a. means per annum (i.e. per year)

The formula is $I = \frac{P \times R \times T}{100}$ $I = \frac{PRT}{100}$

P = Principle (sum of money)
R = Rate of interest
T = Time (in years)
I = Simple interest

Compound interest

In this case the interest is calculated and added to the original sum before the next interest calculation is done.

Compound interest is the interest paid on the total of the original sum of money **and** the interest earned already.

Find the total interest when £250 is invested for 2 years at $8\frac{1}{2}$% compound interest, which is paid annually.

Interest after 1 year = $\frac{250 \times 8 \cdot 5 \times 1}{100}$ = £21·25 $I = \frac{PRT}{100}$

The new sum to be invested = £250 + £21·25 = £271·25

Interest on second year = $\frac{271 \cdot 25 \times 8 \cdot 5 \times 1}{100}$ = £23·06 ← rounded to the nearest penny

The new sum to be invested = £271·25 + £23·06 = £294·31

Compound interest = £294·31 − £250 = £44·31

(continued)

Compound interest (continued)

Doing this over and over again could get a little boring. Fortunately there is a formula for us to use.

$$A = P\left(1 + \frac{R}{100}\right)^n$$

P = Principle (sum of money)
R = Rate of interest
n = Number of years of investment or loan
A = Amount (principle + compound interest after n years)

Converting a table of results into a pie chart

Team results for the Southern Penguins in water-polo games against the Northern Walruses.
Total games played: 14.

Win	Drawn	Lose
9	4	1

← Penguin's results

Convert these results into percentages.
9 ÷ 14 = 0·642 ⟹ 64 % won
4 ÷ 14 = 0·286 ⟹ 29 % drawn
1 ÷ 14 = 0·071 ⟹ 7 % lost

Rounded to the nearest whole number.

We can use these percentages to construct the pie chart.

(Check that the total is **100%**).

Pie chart scales

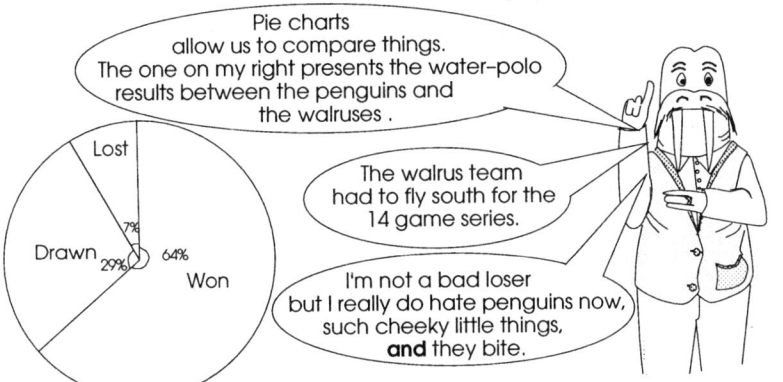

Pie charts allow us to compare things. The one on my right presents the water-polo results between the penguins and the walruses.

Lost 7%
Drawn 29%
Won 64%

The walrus team had to fly south for the 14 game series.

I'm not a bad loser but I really do hate penguins now, such cheeky little things, **and** they bite.

Two way tables

These are often used in science to record data. You usually need to find the total first.

What percentage of the village drive cars?

	Drivers	non-drivers
men	503	57
women	527	51

Find the total number of drivers:

503 + 527 = 1030

Find the total number of people:

503 + 57 + 527 + 51 = 1138

1030 ÷ 1138 = 0·905 096 7

Convert to a percentage.

so 91% of the village drive (to the nearest whole %)
(Check the question to see how accurate the answer needs to be).

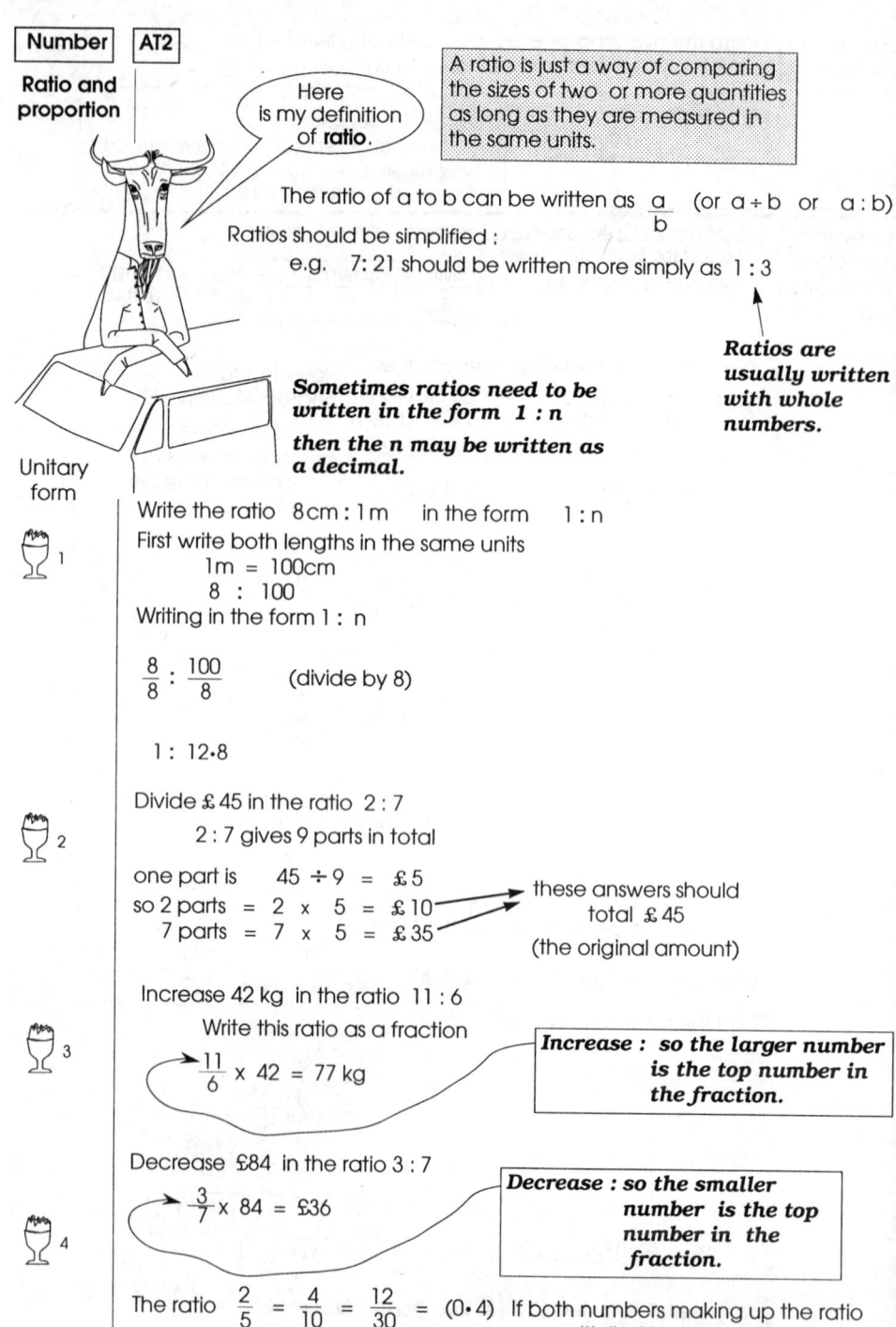

Number — AT2

Ratio and proportion

*Here is my definition of **ratio**.*

A ratio is just a way of comparing the sizes of two or more quantities as long as they are measured in the same units.

The ratio of a to b can be written as $\frac{a}{b}$ (or $a \div b$ or $a : b$)

Ratios should be simplified:
  e.g. 7 : 21 should be written more simply as 1 : 3

Ratios are usually written with whole numbers.

Sometimes ratios need to be written in the form **1 : n** then the n may be written as a decimal.

Unitary form

1
Write the ratio 8 cm : 1 m in the form 1 : n
First write both lengths in the same units
  1 m = 100 cm
  8 : 100
Writing in the form 1 : n

$\frac{8}{8} : \frac{100}{8}$ (divide by 8)

1 : 12·8

2
Divide £45 in the ratio 2 : 7
  2 : 7 gives 9 parts in total
one part is   45 ÷ 9 = £5
so 2 parts = 2 × 5 = £10
   7 parts = 7 × 5 = £35

these answers should total £45 (the original amount)

3
Increase 42 kg in the ratio 11 : 6
  Write this ratio as a fraction
  $\frac{11}{6} \times 42 = 77$ kg

Increase : so the larger number is the top number in the fraction.

4
Decrease £84 in the ratio 3 : 7
  $\frac{3}{7} \times 84 = £36$

Decrease : so the smaller number is the top number in the fraction.

The ratio $\frac{2}{5} = \frac{4}{10} = \frac{12}{30} = (0 \cdot 4)$ If both numbers making up the ratio are multiplied by the same number the ratio remains unchanged.

- 21 -

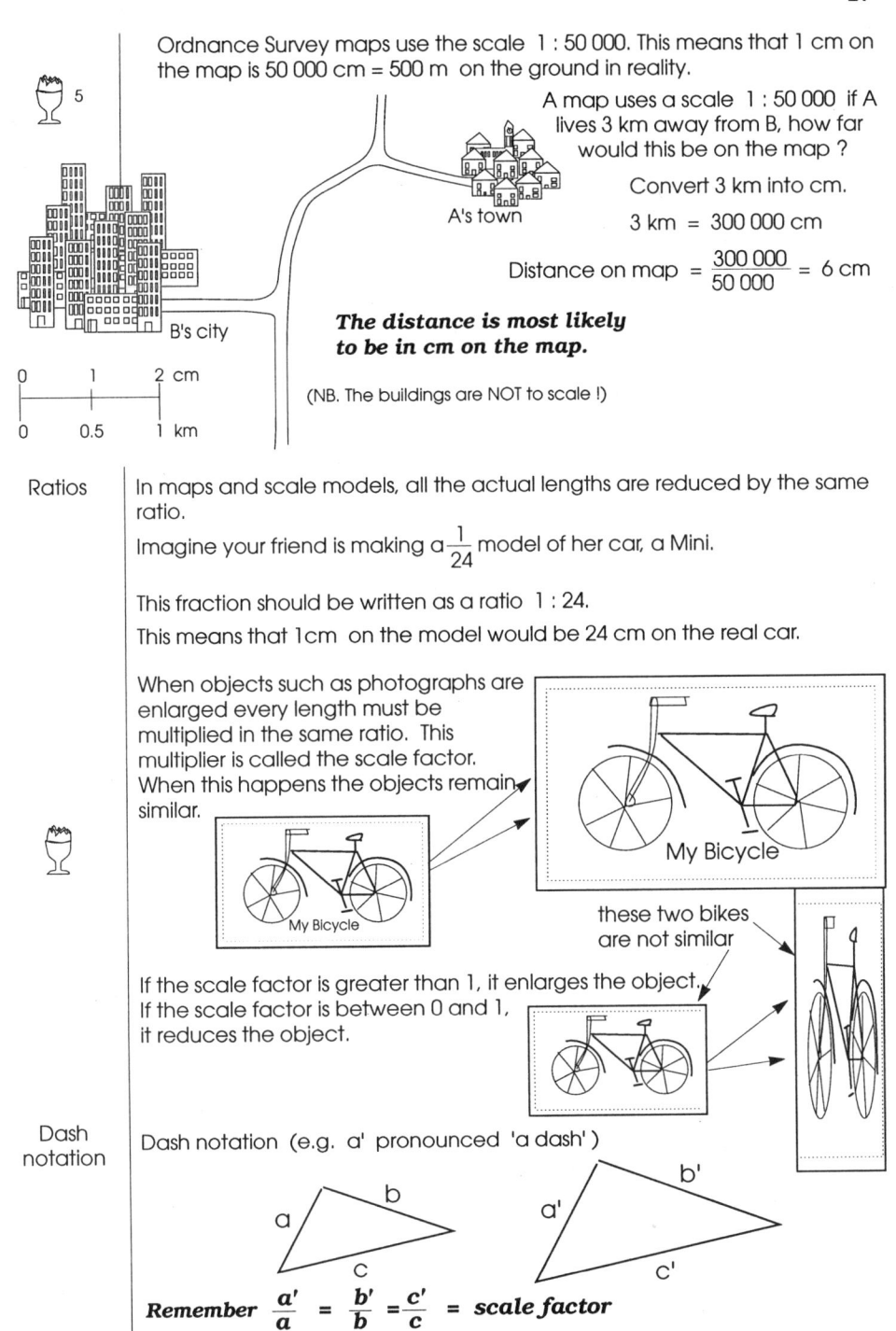

Ordnance Survey maps use the scale 1 : 50 000. This means that 1 cm on the map is 50 000 cm = 500 m on the ground in reality.

A map uses a scale 1 : 50 000 if A lives 3 km away from B, how far would this be on the map ?

Convert 3 km into cm.

A's town   3 km = 300 000 cm

Distance on map = $\frac{300\,000}{50\,000}$ = 6 cm

B's city

The distance is most likely to be in cm on the map.

(NB. The buildings are NOT to scale !)

0 1 2 cm
0 0.5 1 km

Ratios | In maps and scale models, all the actual lengths are reduced by the same ratio.
Imagine your friend is making a $\frac{1}{24}$ model of her car, a Mini.

This fraction should be written as a ratio 1 : 24.
This means that 1cm on the model would be 24 cm on the real car.

When objects such as photographs are enlarged every length must be multiplied in the same ratio. This multiplier is called the scale factor. When this happens the objects remain similar.

My Bicycle

My Bicycle

these two bikes are not similar

If the scale factor is greater than 1, it enlarges the object.
If the scale factor is between 0 and 1, it reduces the object.

Dash notation | Dash notation (e.g. a' pronounced 'a dash')

a, b, c

a', b', c'

Remember $\frac{a'}{a} = \frac{b'}{b} = \frac{c'}{c}$ = *scale factor*

Number — AT2

Ratios and recipes

Ratios can also be a way of explaining the quantities to be used in a mixture.
Punch can made from wine, lemonade and fruit juice, in the ratio 2 to 5 to 1.
How much do you need of each ingredient for 6 litres of punch?

Ratio of 2 : 5 : 1 gives a total of 8 parts:

Wine needed $= \frac{2}{8} \times 6$ litres $= 1 \cdot 5$ litres

Lemonade needed $= \frac{5}{8} \times 6$ litres $= 3 \cdot 75$ litres

Fruit juice needed $= \frac{1}{8} \times 6$ litres $= 0 \cdot 75$ litres

N.B. Check that our total is the same as the total given in the question by adding them together.
i.e. $1 \cdot 5 + 3 \cdot 75 + 0 \cdot 75 = 6$

Connection between fractions and ratios

Watch out for trick questions like this:
If $\frac{1}{3}$ of the maths class is girls, what is the ratio of girls to boys?

The fraction $\frac{1}{3}$ means that the class has been shared into three parts altogether.
1 of these 3 parts is girls so the boys must be $3 - 1 = 2$ parts
Ratio of girls to boys is $1 : 2$ ⟵ 1 : 2 means $1 + 2 = 3$ parts altogether and 1 of these 3 ($\frac{1}{3}$) is girls.

Direct proportion

> If 2 quantities are in direct proportion then their ratio must stay the same even when the quantities are increased or decreased.

Mary uses a drink recipe using 3 parts orange juice to 7 parts lemonade.
To make a drink for herself she uses   3 fl. oz. orange juice
                                        7 fl. oz. lemonade

If she makes enough for 4 people   *fl. oz. means fluid ounces.*
she must multiply both quantities by 4.   **20 fl. oz. = 1 pint**

Orange juice $= 3 \times 4 = 12$ fl. oz.
Lemonade $= 7 \times 4 = 28$ fl. oz.

Inverse proportion

> 2 quantities are in inverse proportion when one quantity increases at the same rate as the other quantity decreases.

10 tins of cat food will feed my 2 cats for 5 days. How many days would the same number of tins feed 4 cats?

This will feed 2 cats for 5 days.
The same food will feed 4 cats for $5 \div 2 = 2 \cdot 5$ days

4 is 2 x 2
so divide by 2 here

⟵ Do check that your answer makes sense. Your answer should give a shorter time because there are more cats to feed.

Solving numerical problems using mixed units.

Rates

Here are two examples

The rate at which something occurs involves comparing one measurement with another – the second one is usually a unit quantity.

A bath filling at **18 litres/minute** has 18 litres of water pouring into it every minute.

A car travelling at **47 miles/hour** (m.p.h.) will travel 47 miles if it continues at this speed, for one hour.

If the rate does not alter then the graph of the event will be a straight line.

i.e. per minute, per hour, per day etc.

Graphs and constant rates

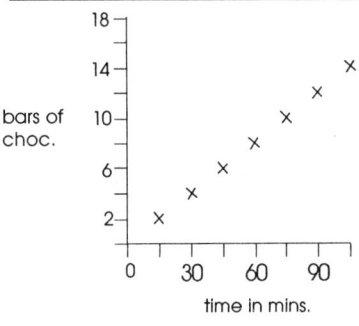

A graph showing the number of bars consumed at different times after the start

bars of choc.

time in mins.

Unwisely, Sheep has been pigging on chocolate at the rate of 2 bars/15 min. The straight line graph tells the story.

the gradient of the graph $= \frac{2}{15}$ i.e. 8 bars per hour.

If £9 is the same as 85 French Francs, then the exchange rate can be thought of as $\frac{£9}{FF85}$ = 0·106 £ per FF (correct to 3 d.p.)

or $\frac{FF85}{£9}$ = 9·444 FF per £ (correct to 3 d.p.)

Exchange rate

Use this conversion rate to change £79·50 into FF

£79·50 = 79·50 × $\frac{85}{9}$

= 750·83 FF

| Number | AT2 |

Graphs and constant rates continued

Constant rates can change from time to time e.g. the bath taps can be turned on fully for a while and then altered to a slower flow rate. Abrupt changes like this would give a graph with a series of straight lines.

Graph showing the rate at which a bath fills with water

(Litres of water vs Time in minutes; points approximately at (1,30), (2,50), (3,65), (4,80), (5,88), (6,90), (7,90))

During 0 – 2 minutes: the bath filled at $\frac{50}{2}$ = 25 litres/min.

During 2 – 4 minutes: the bath filled at $\frac{30}{2}$ = 15 litres/min.

During 4 – 7 minutes: the bath filled at $\frac{10}{3}$ = 3·3 litres/min.

Average rates

The average rate for filling the bath = $\frac{\text{total amount of water}}{\text{total time taken}} = \frac{90}{7}$

= 12·9 litres/min.

More on average rates

Some things vary so quickly that it is quite impossible, or very difficult, to give the rate as a constant, e.g. cars rarely maintain a constant speed, road conditions and other vehicles affect the speed.

Remember to convert minutes into a decimal of an hour e.g.
15 min = $\frac{15}{60}$ = 0·25

A car travels 85 miles in 2 hours 15 mins.
Find the average speed.

Average speed = $\frac{85 \text{ miles}}{2 \cdot 25 \text{ hrs.}}$ = 37·77777 = 37·8 m.p.h.
(correct to 3 sig. fig.)

N.B.

People can get confused about what is divided by what. If this happens to you, do have a look at the units because they tell you exactly what to do.

For example,

litres per minute can be written as litres / min or $\frac{\text{litres}}{\text{min.}}$

So if we travel 30 miles in 2 hours and look for the speed in miles per hour

we need $\frac{30 \text{ miles}}{2 \text{ hrs.}}$ = 15 m/h (15 mph)

Converting units

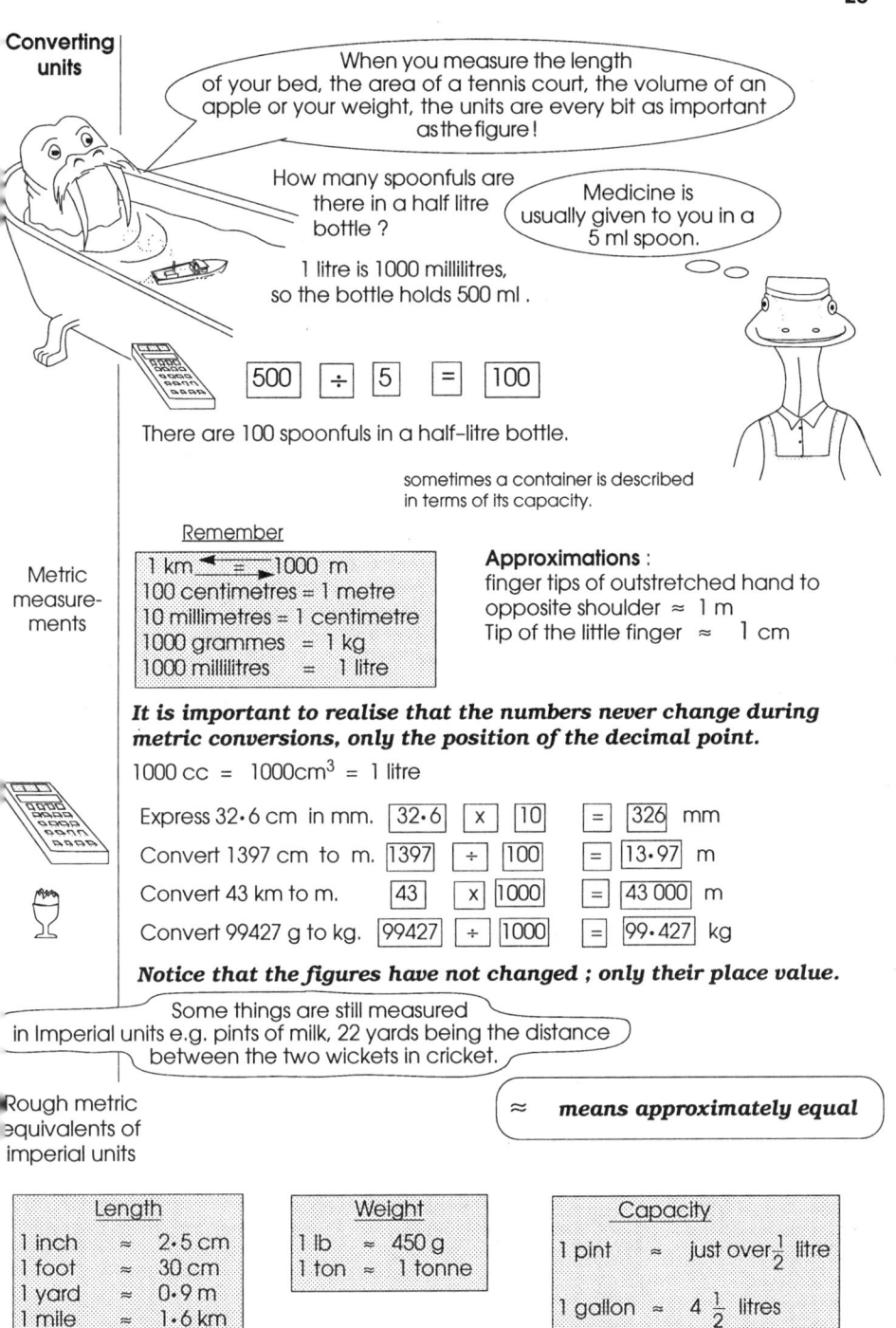

When you measure the length of your bed, the area of a tennis court, the volume of an apple or your weight, the units are every bit as important as the figure!

How many spoonfuls are there in a half litre bottle?

Medicine is usually given to you in a 5 ml spoon.

1 litre is 1000 millilitres, so the bottle holds 500 ml.

$500 \div 5 = 100$

There are 100 spoonfuls in a half-litre bottle.

sometimes a container is described in terms of its capacity.

Remember

Metric measurements

1 km = 1000 m
100 centimetres = 1 metre
10 millimetres = 1 centimetre
1000 grammes = 1 kg
1000 millilitres = 1 litre

Approximations:
finger tips of outstretched hand to opposite shoulder ≈ 1 m
Tip of the little finger ≈ 1 cm

It is important to realise that the numbers never change during metric conversions, only the position of the decimal point.

1000 cc = 1000 cm³ = 1 litre

Express 32·6 cm in mm. $32·6 \times 10 = 326$ mm
Convert 1397 cm to m. $1397 \div 100 = 13·97$ m
Convert 43 km to m. $43 \times 1000 = 43\,000$ m
Convert 99427 g to kg. $99427 \div 1000 = 99·427$ kg

Notice that the figures have not changed; only their place value.

Some things are still measured in Imperial units e.g. pints of milk, 22 yards being the distance between the two wickets in cricket.

Rough metric equivalents of imperial units

≈ means approximately equal

Length	
1 inch	≈ 2·5 cm
1 foot	≈ 30 cm
1 yard	≈ 0·9 m
1 mile	≈ 1·6 km

Weight	
1 lb	≈ 450 g
1 ton	≈ 1 tonne

Capacity	
1 pint	≈ just over $\frac{1}{2}$ litre
1 gallon	≈ $4\frac{1}{2}$ litres

Number | **AT2** | Any measurement that is made relies on the accuracy of the instrument used – in other words, **all measurements are approximate**. Just choose whatever is appropriate for the situation.

"My friend lives 5 km away." This really means that the distance is somewhere between 4·5 km and 5·5 km.

Mark can run 100 m in 10.28 secs.

This means that the actual time was somewhere between 10.275 and 10.285 seconds.

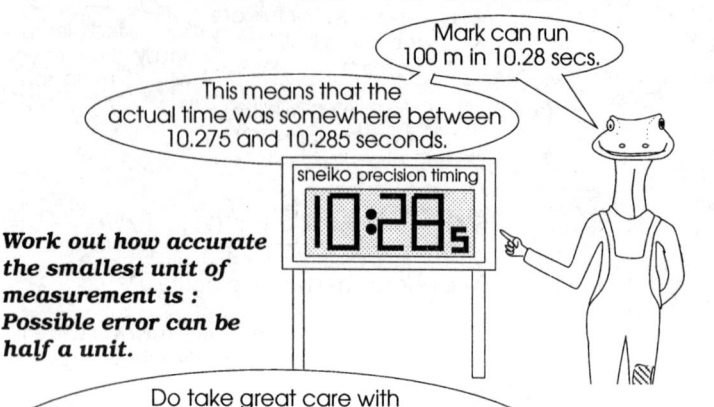

sneiko precision timing

10:28 s

Work out how accurate the smallest unit of measurement is : Possible error can be half a unit.

Do take great care with units when you are doing calculations. Some questions use several different units and it is important to spot this, convert everything to the same units and then do the calculation.

Mixed units

I've given some examples below.

Find the perimeter of this shape.

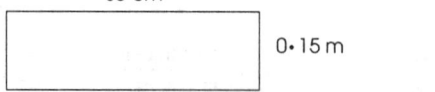

50 cm

0·15 m

Make sure that you convert all measurements to the same units.

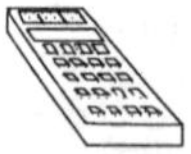

50 cm = 0·5 m

| 0·5 m | + | 0·15 m | + | 0·5 m | + | 0·15 m | = | 1·3 m |

or 0·15 m = 15 cm   so   15 cm + 50 cm + 15 cm + 50 cm = 130 cm

Find the area of this window.

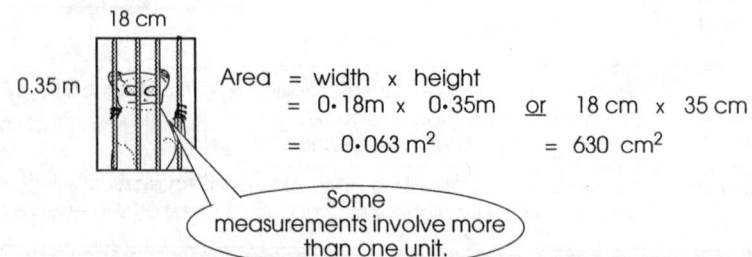

18 cm

0.35 m

Area = width × height
     = 0·18m × 0·35m   or   18 cm × 35 cm
     = 0·063 m^2 = 630 cm^2

Some measurements involve more than one unit.

Compound measures

1 & 2

A car travels at 30 m.p.h. (miles per hour). This means that the car would cover 30 miles in 1 hour if it continued at that speed.

A lump of lead has a density of 13·6 g per cm^3.
With density we are comparing the mass per unit volume.

This 'per unit volume' just means for every unit of volume (e.g. for each cubic centimetre)

N.B.

Where units contain a / sign e.g. m/s, the / means that the first unit has been divided by the second unit (it means the same as per).
Mark runs 100 m in 10·28 secs. His speed is 100 ÷ 10·28 = 9·728 m/s.
= 9·728 m per second.

Time, clocks, a.m. and p.m.

A clock with 1 to 12 on the face doesn't know if it is morning (a.m.) or afternoon (p.m.)

Midnight   Midday   Midnight
             a.m.   p.m.

24 hour clock — Most train and bus timetables (and digital watches) have a 24 hour system.

Midnight   Midday   Midnight
0000   1200   2400

'See you at 6 O'Clock' can mean two times, → 6·00 am or 6·00 pm
'See you at 1800 hours' means only one time.

e.g Convert 4·35 pm to 24 hour clock.
     4·35 + 12 = 16·35

The full stop can be left out   16·35 = 1635

Calculations

How long is it from 0150 to 0320 ?

0150	to	0200	is	10 mins.
0200	to	0300	is	1 hour
0300	to	0320	is	20 mins.

Which totals to 1 hour 30 minutes.

Put away your calculator (it doesn't understand that there are 60 mins in an hour) . . . . and use this method:

Timetables

Using the 24 hour clock removes one of the ways that mistakes can occur and so they are used for timetables. Using timetables is really a matter of common sense, though often, good eyesight is important because so much information is given on each page.

Calendar

30 days hath September, April, June and November. All the rest have 31, except February alone which has 28 clear and 29 in each leap year.

Number | **AT 2**

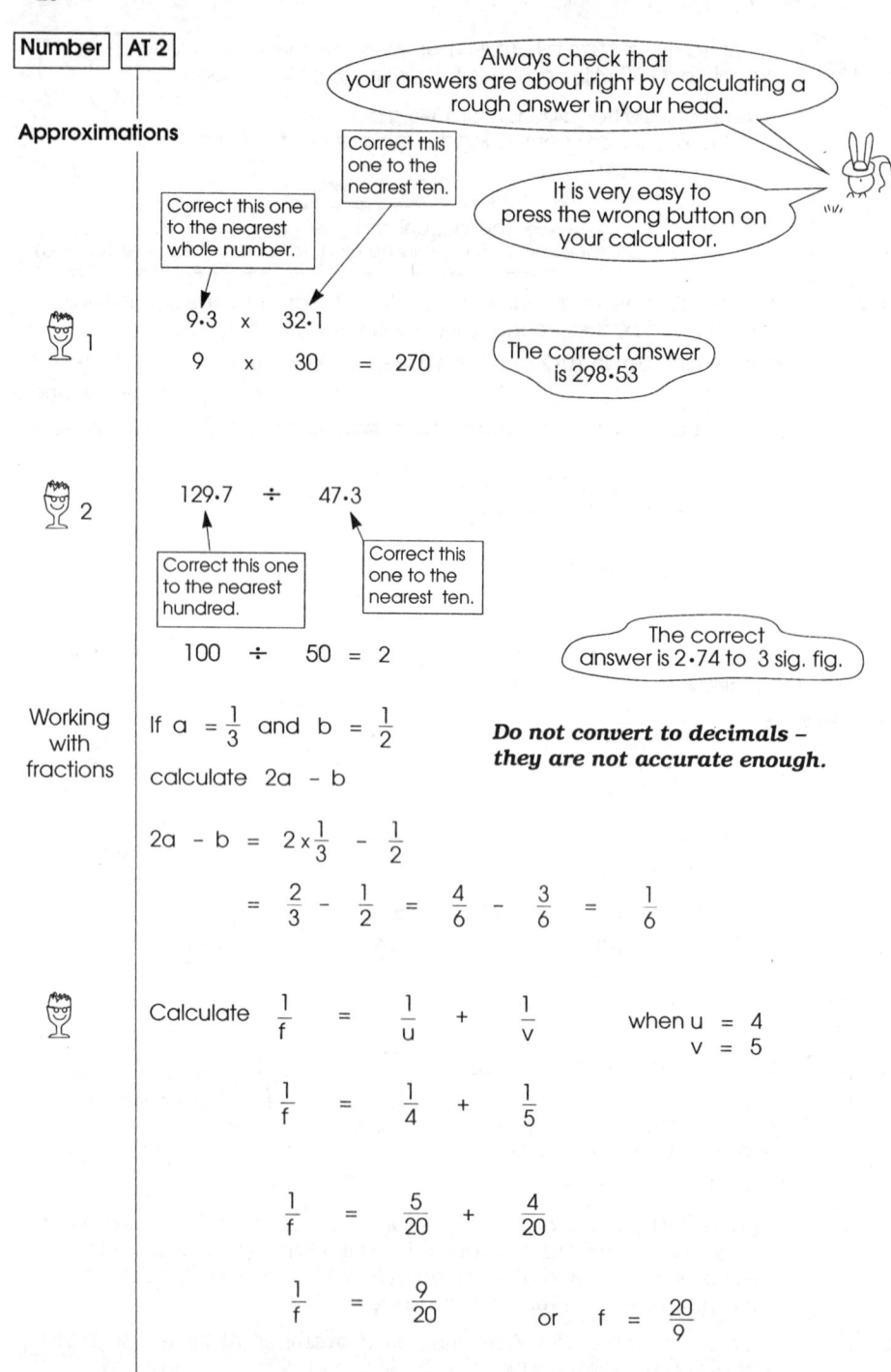

Approximations

> Always check that your answers are about right by calculating a rough answer in your head.
>
> It is very easy to press the wrong button on your calculator.

1

9·3 × 32·1

9 × 30 = 270

Correct this one to the nearest whole number. (9.3)
Correct this one to the nearest ten. (32.1)

> The correct answer is 298·53

2

129·7 ÷ 47·3

Correct this one to the nearest hundred. (129.7)
Correct this one to the nearest ten. (47.3)

100 ÷ 50 = 2

> The correct answer is 2·74 to 3 sig. fig.

Working with fractions

If $a = \frac{1}{3}$ and $b = \frac{1}{2}$ calculate $2a - b$

Do not convert to decimals – they are not accurate enough.

$$2a - b = 2 \times \frac{1}{3} - \frac{1}{2}$$

$$= \frac{2}{3} - \frac{1}{2} = \frac{4}{6} - \frac{3}{6} = \frac{1}{6}$$

Calculate $\frac{1}{f} = \frac{1}{u} + \frac{1}{v}$ when $u = 4$, $v = 5$

$$\frac{1}{f} = \frac{1}{4} + \frac{1}{5}$$

$$\frac{1}{f} = \frac{5}{20} + \frac{4}{20}$$

$$\frac{1}{f} = \frac{9}{20} \quad \text{or} \quad f = \frac{20}{9}$$

Exponential decay

> If you repeatedly multiply a number by a quantity less than 1, you get exponential decay. The quantity gets smaller and smaller but never reaches 0.

A population of forest birds decreases by 10% each year because of loss of habitat. At the end of each year it is 90% (or 0·9) of what it was at the beginning of the year. The population began at 50 000. What will the population be after 10 years?

50 000 × 0·9 × 0·9 × 0·9 . . .

(because it's 10 years)

It is quicker to write 50 000 × 0.9^{10} = 17 433·922
= 17 400 to 3 sig. figs.

In the case of forest birds the population might reach 0 for biological reasons i.e. the breeding population becomes too small.

Exponential growth

> A quantity which grows by being multiplied by the same number (greater than 1) in equal periods of time is said to grow **exponentially**.

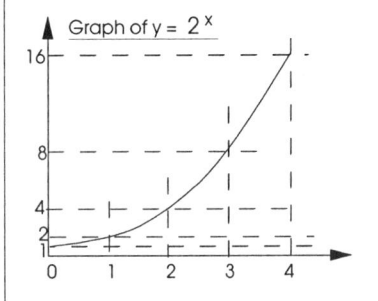

Graph of $y = 2^x$

When you start work ask for
1p on the first day,
2 × 1p = 2p on the second day
and so on. In other words, the pay doubles each new day.

Work out how much you would earn on day 30.

Algebra

Variables

> Algebra is using letters or symbols in place of numbers or quantities.

> When a letter represents different numerical values it is called a variable.

1

If t = temperature in °C at 3 pm each day,

t = 20   t = 24   t = 23 might be the temperature on three days in July.

The use of variables enables us to write down general expressions, equations and formulae for ideas or patterns in the physical world.

Sequences

> A list of numbers which is produced by following the same rule repeatedly is called a sequence.

Computers are very efficient at generating sequences because they can be programmed to keep following the same rule repeatedly.

> The rule is usually easy to work out if we label each number in the list with its position.

the dots mean there are lots more terms to come.

3, 6, 9, 12 ...

Position:	1st	2nd	3rd	4th	...	nth
Term:	3	6	9	12		
Difference	+3	+3	+3			

> We'll come back to this one on the next page.

Find the next 2 terms, the nth and the 20th term of the sequence -1, 4, 9, 14 ...

2

Position:	1st	2nd	3rd	4th	...	nth
Term:	-1	4	9	14		
Difference		5	5	5		

The next two terms are 14 + 5 = 19
and 19 + 5 = 24

the nth term = 5n + ?

common difference   position

5 x 1 = 5   we require -1   5 − 6 = **-1**
5 x 2 = 10   we require 4   10 − 6 = **4**

$\Longrightarrow$ the nth term = 5n − 6

To find the 20th term substitute 20 in place of n.

20th term = 5 x 20 − 6 = 94

If the differences are equal we can find any term by multiplying n by the difference and then adding or subtracting a number.

minus 6 is what we need to do here

General rule for investigations.

When you are asked to find a rule for a set of numbers you have obtained in an investigation it is a good idea to find the general rule in algebraic terms as well as describing it in words.

Return to 3, 6, 9, 12...

🥚 1

Find the nth term in the sequence 3, 6, 9, 12...

Position: 1st 2nd 3rd 4th ... n^{th}
Term: 3   6   9   12
Difference   +3   +3   +3

3n gives   3 × 1 = **3**   3 × 2 = **6**   3 × 3 = **9**

↑ difference   ↑ position of the term

so   3n + 0 = 3n   3n is the nth term.

Some practice for you

Find the next 2 terms, the nth term and the 50th term in the sequence 19, 15, 11, 7, ...

The answers are at the end of this section on page 32

≷ Solving the next type of problem is easier if you have square numbers at your fingertips. ≷

$1^2 = 1$ $2^2 = 4$ $3^2 = 9$ $4^2 = 16$ etc. or

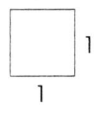

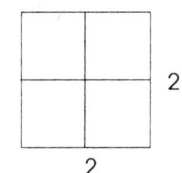

🥚 2

Find the nth term and hence* the 10th term in the sequence 5, 9, 15, 23 ...

Position: 1st 2nd 3rd 4th ... n^{th}

* **hence means use what you have just found out.**

Term: 5   9   15   23

1st Difference   4   6   8   ←── **If this row of differences are not equal then write down a set of 2nd differences.**

2nd Difference   2   2

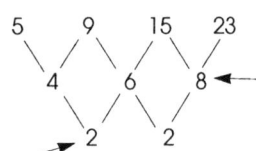

This 2nd set of differences are equal which implies that the nth term contains a n^2 term.

An expression with a n^2 term is called a quadratic.

So; following the pattern: n^{th} term = n^2 + ?

1st term = 5 = 1^2 + 4 = 1^2 + 1 + 3
2nd term = 9 = 2^2 + 5 = 2^2 + 2 + 3
3rd term = 15 = 3^2 + 6 = 3^2 + 3 + 3
n^{th} term = n^2 + n + 3

check by working out the 4th term
$23 = 4^2 + 4 + 3$
$= 16 + 4 + 3$
$= 23$ ← correct !

🥚 3

Find the next 2 terms and the nth term of the sequence 5, 10, 17, 26 ...

(a harder example)

(continued overleaf but try it now before turning the page)

Algebra continued 3

The sequence is 5, 10, 17, 26 ...

Position: 1st 2nd 3rd 4th ... nth

Term: 5 10 17 26

1st Difference   5   7   9

2nd Difference   2   2   **N.B.** '2' again $\Rightarrow n^2$

Now you complete this answer.

So; following the pattern: nth term = n^2 + ?

1st term = 5 = $1^2 + 4$ = $1^2 + 2 \times 1 + 2$
2nd term = 10 = $2^2 + 6$ =
3rd term = 17 =
nth term =

So the 5th term =

and the 6th term =
                = 50

The rule is nth term = $n^2 + 2n + 2$

> The answers to question 1 on page 31 are:
> 3 and −1, 15 − 4n or −4n + 15, −185

Formulae and Equations

In this section we are going to look at equations but using letters in place of numbers.

We are also going to concentrate on keeping the equations balanced.

If I give a shopkeeper £1 for 3 Wispas costing 17p each, how much change do I get?

Change = 100 − (3 x 17)
       = 100 − 51
       = 49 pence

£1 = 100p   We must use the same units.

Suppose I buy 2 Wispas at y pence each. What change do I need? In sorting this one out we follow exactly the same steps as we did in the last question. Let c = change (in pence)

C = 100 − 2 x y
C = 100 − 2 y

Remember that in this sort of work we assume the multiplication sign, e.g. 2 y means 2 multiplied by y

Words to formula

Substituting into formulae

More usually instructions are given using letters instead of words. The formula for the time taken (t) for a bus journey could be written like this: t = 16 + 2b

where b is the number of stops. t is the time in minutes

How long would I take if I went 3 stops ?

t = 16 + 2 x 3
t =   22

so I took 22 minutes.

Do remember to multiply 2 and 3 before you do the adding.

The general rule is to do brackets first, then powers (e.g. y^2), then do any multiplications and divisions, then do the adding and subtracting.

1

The area A of a trapezium can be found by using the formula

$$A = \frac{1}{2}(a + b)h$$

a and b are the lengths of the parallel sides.
h is the perpendicular distance between a and b.

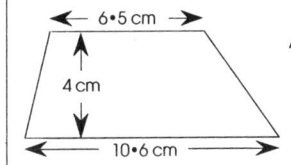

6•5 cm
4 cm
10•6 cm

$$A = \frac{1}{2}(10{\cdot}6 + 6{\cdot}5) \times 4$$

$$A = 34 \text{ cm}^2$$

2

$V = \frac{1}{4} x^2 h$ find h when V = 20 and x = 12

$\Rightarrow$ $20 = \frac{1}{4} \times 12 \times 12 \times h$

$\Rightarrow$ $20 = 36h$

You could rearrange first but it is usually easier to substitute values and then solve the equation.

$\Rightarrow$ $\frac{\cancel{20}^5}{\cancel{36}_9} = h$

$\Rightarrow$ $h = \frac{5}{9}$

Substituting using fractions

$v = ut + \frac{1}{2}at^2$ Find V when u = 0, $t = 9\frac{1}{3}$ and a = 10

$v = 0 \times 9\frac{1}{3} + \frac{1}{2} \times 10 \times (9\frac{1}{3})^2$

Ans. $435 \frac{5}{9}$

Your key strokes will depend upon which type of calculator you are using. If you have one with a fraction button $\boxed{a^b/_c}$ do learn to use it.

The answer is as a fraction because the question contains a fraction.

Don't use the $\boxed{x^2}$ button if you are multiplying fractions. Most calculators convert fractions into decimals if you do so.

Algebra

Reciprocal

Any number multiplied by its reciprocal gives 1 as the answer.

A reciprocal is the number you get when you divide 1 by the number or expression.

e.g. The reciprocal of 5 is $\frac{1}{5}$

The reciprocal of $1\frac{1}{3}$ is $\frac{3}{4}$ (why?)

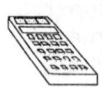

Because $1\frac{1}{3} = \frac{4}{3}$ and

the reciprocal of $\frac{4}{3} = \frac{3}{4}$

We are having a second look at reciprocals, they are relevant to both number and algebra.

The $\boxed{\frac{1}{x}}$ button will perform this task but the display will be in decimal form.

Flow charts

Flow charts are diagrams that represent instructions. These instructions are given in rectangular boxes, and questions are given in diamond-shaped boxes

The questions require a decision from you. Once you have made the decision you follow either the yes or no arrow. Remember to write down the answers for each step of the process.

This is a fairly **rough** guide for changing temperature in °C into °F, and vice versa.

Follow the flow chart to convert 21 °C to °F.

Write down the answer at each step, i.e. 21, 42, 74 . . :

Answer = 74 °F.

Flow chart:
- Start
- write down the temperature
- is it in °C
  - Yes → × 2 → + 32 → write down the answer
  - No → − 32 → ÷ 2 → write down the answer
- Stop

Solving equations	Equations are balancing puzzles.	The diagram shows a set of scales. Use x for the weight of a tin.

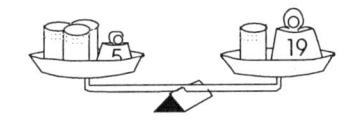

$$x + x + x + 5 = x + 19$$
$$x + x + 5 = 19 \quad \text{(subtract x from each side)}$$
$$2x = 14 \quad \text{(subtract 5 from each side)}$$
$$x = 7$$

Substituting into a formula and then solving an equation	This is a **formula**. If $v = 7$, $u = 3$ and $s = 5$, when they are substituted into the formula an equation results. i.e. Only one letter is unknown.

$$v^2 - u^2 = 2as$$
$$7^2 - 3^2 = 2 \times a \times 5$$
$$49 - 9 = 10a$$
$$40 = 10a$$
$$\frac{40}{10} = \frac{10a}{10}$$
$$4 = a$$

We want to find the value of a, so we divide **both** sides by 10.

Solving harder equations	

$$3 = 27 - 5p \quad \boxed{-27}$$
$$-24 = -5p$$
$$\frac{-24}{-5} = p \quad \boxed{\div -5}$$
$$4\tfrac{4}{5} = p \text{ or } 4 \cdot 8 = p$$

If you are solving a 'real life' problem you may have to round off a decimal but it is safer to express your answer as a fraction.

Another problem, a different method

$$4 \cdot 6 - 2 \cdot 5q = 6 \quad \boxed{+2 \cdot 5q}$$
$$4 \cdot 6 = 6 + 2 \cdot 5q \quad \boxed{-6}$$
$$-1 \cdot 4 = 2 \cdot 5q$$
$$-0 \cdot 56 = q \quad \boxed{\div 2 \cdot 5}$$

There are decimals in this question so you should give your answer as a decimal.

<u>N.B.</u> Check your answer by substituting your value for x back in the question.

$$\boxed{27} \; \boxed{-} \; \boxed{5} \; \boxed{\times} \; \boxed{4 \cdot 8} \; \boxed{=}$$
$$\boxed{4 \cdot 6} \; \boxed{-} \; \boxed{2 \cdot 5} \; \boxed{\times} \; \boxed{0 \cdot 56} \; \boxed{^+/_-} \; \boxed{=}$$

Do you get the same answer that was given in your question? If not, think for a moment and then try again.

Algebra

Solving equations

This business of rearranging equations and formulae caused me a lot of problems and I only really sorted it out by trying quite hard and by asking my teacher for help when I got stuck.

Having an unknown on both sides.

We need x to be on one side only

Solve $\quad 1 - 3x = x + 7$

$1 - 3x + 3x = x + 7 + 3x \quad$ Eliminate the smaller x term, in this case −3x, by adding 3x to both sides.

$1 = 4x + 7$

Check your answer.
$1 - 3 \times -1 \cdot 5 = -1 \cdot 5 + 7$

Have a go at finishing this.

1

$5(x - 3) = 4(3 - x)$
$5x - 15 = 12 - 4x \quad$ multiply out the brackets
$9x - 15 = 12 \quad$ add 4x to both sides
$9x = 27 \quad$ add 15 to both sides
$x = 3$

Add or subtract the inverse of the lower x term if there is an x term on both sides.

2

$\dfrac{x - 2}{10} = \dfrac{x}{4} + 1 \quad$ The lowest common denominator is 20 so × both sides by 20

$\Rightarrow \quad 20\left(\dfrac{x-2}{10}\right) = 20\left(\dfrac{x}{4} + 1\right)$

$\Rightarrow \quad 2x - 4 = 5x + 20 \quad$ −2x from both sides
$\quad\quad\quad\; -4 = 3x + 20 \quad$ −20 from both sides
$\quad\quad -24 = 3x \quad\quad\quad\; \div 3 \;$ both sides
$\quad\quad\;\; -8 = x$

Some for you to solve

In each case check your answer by substituting back into the question.

(1) $\quad \dfrac{x}{9} - 8 = -6$

(2) $\quad x^2 + 1 = 19$

Use your calculator to solve these types of equations using the x^2 and $\sqrt{\;}$ keys.

(3) $\quad \sqrt{x} = 11 \cdot 3$

If you have to round off remember it's 3 sig. figs. unless told otherwise.

Rearranging formulae

This is a lot like solving equations. We have to keep both sides balanced and carefully 'unwrap' the letter which has to be made the subject (i.e. left on its own on one side).

1

$V = lbh$

Make l the subject.

This is the formula for the volume of a cuboid :
(product of 3 lengths $\Rightarrow$ vol)

$\Rightarrow \dfrac{V}{bh} = \dfrac{lbh}{bh} \quad \div$ by bh

$\Rightarrow \dfrac{V}{bh} = l$

2

Rearrange $a = \sqrt{b} - c$ to give b in terms of a and c.

$\Rightarrow a + c = \sqrt{b} \quad + c$

$\Rightarrow (a + c)^2 = b \quad$ square

$(a + c)(a + c) = b$

simplify or leave bracket squared.

$a^2 + 2ac + c^2 = b$

Trial and Improvement Methods

Equations may have the unknown quantity raised to a power.

3

Find z if $z^3 = 30$

and we can find the value of the unknown by trial and improvement.

Mmmm! let me think about this...

$3 \times 3 \times 3 = 27$
$4 \times 4 \times 4 = 64$

Ponder Ponder! z must lie somewhere between 3 and 4 i.e. 3.something.

I'll just have to start guessing now.

try $3 \cdot 1 \times 3 \cdot 1 \times 3 \cdot 1 = 29 \cdot 791$

so 3.1 is not big enough

try $3 \cdot 2 \times 3 \cdot 2 \times 3 \cdot 2 = 32 \cdot 768 \quad$ 3.2 is too big

try $3 \cdot 11 \times 3 \cdot 11 \times 3 \cdot 11 = 30 \cdot 080231$

So $z = 3 \cdot 1$ is closest correct to 2 sig. figs.

Do check that you have found a solution to the correct number of figures or decimal places asked for.

Algebra — Find a positive value of x if $x^3 - 2x = 2$ (answer correct to 2 d.p.)

Drawing a graph of $y = x^3 - 2x$ for values of $x \geq 0$ will help to give a rough idea of the solution.

You will need a table of values for y.

'solution' is just another word for answer e.g. find the solution.

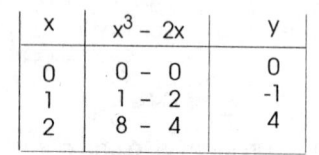

x	$x^3 - 2x$	y
0	0 − 0	0
1	1 − 2	−1
2	8 − 4	4

There is an example of a different way of setting out this type of table a few pages further on.

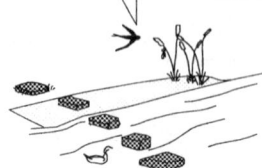

$y = 2$ here

So a solution lies between $x = 1$ and $x = 2$

The 'too big', 'too small', comments are an important part of your answer.

You must now substitute your first guess in the expression $x^3 - 2x$ to make it ≈ 2

Try x = 1·7 |1·7| |x^y| |3| |−| |2| |x| |1·7| |=| 1·513   too small

Try x = 1·8 $1·8^3$ − 2 x 1·8 = 2·232   too big

Try x = 1·76 $1·76^3$ − 2 x 1·76 = 1·932   too small

Try x = 1·77 $1·77^3$ − 2 x 1·77 = 2·005

so x = 1·77 is the best positive solution.

Always calculate at least one value above and one value below the result you need.

Algebraic Manipulation

If you add 3a to 4a, the result is 7a i.e. 3a + 4a = 7a.
We can add the 3a and 4a because they are like terms.
We cannot add 3a and 4b in this way because they are not like terms.
We call this process of adding like terms 'simplifying'.

Collecting like terms

Simplify   7p − 3q + 2p   Answer = 9p − 3q
Simplify   2ab + 3bc − 4ba − b^2
Answer = 3bc − 2ab − b^2 (only the terms in ab are like terms)
Remember we usually arrange the letters in a term in alphabetical order.

Algebraic Manipulation

> The list of basic techniques
> Simplifying
> Adding fractions
> Solving equations
> Dealing with brackets
> Rearranging formulae and Substitution

You do need to have these basic techniques at your fingertips.

Whenever you have trouble using algebra try to get around the difficulty by thinking how you would do it with numbers.

Simplifying Multiplication

$$\frac{3b^2}{20} \times \frac{25}{9b}$$

$$\Rightarrow \frac{\overset{1}{\cancel{3b^2}}}{\underset{4}{\cancel{20}}} \times \frac{\overset{5}{\cancel{25}}}{\underset{3}{\cancel{9b}}} = \frac{5b}{12}$$

Remember that if you divide, you must change ÷ to × and write the reciprocal of the second term.

Division

$$16x^2y \div \frac{2x}{5y} = 16x^2y \times \frac{5y}{2x} = 40xy^2$$

Simplifying indices

$$4x^4 \times 3x^2 = 4 \times x \times x \times x \times x \times 3 \times x \times x$$
$$= 12x^6$$

$$10y^3 \div 4y = \frac{\cancel{2} \times 5 \times \cancel{y} \times y \times y}{\cancel{2} \times 2 \times \cancel{y}}$$

$$= \frac{5y^2}{2}$$

$$(5x^3)^2 = 5x^3 \times 5x^3 = 25x^6$$

The rules here are fairly simple:

to multiply $\Longrightarrow$ add the indices

to divide $\Longrightarrow$ subtract the indices

Adding fractions

$$\frac{9q}{2} + \frac{6q}{5}$$

we need a denominator of 2 × 5

$$\frac{9q \times 5}{2 \times 5} + \frac{6q \times 2}{5 \times 2}$$

we have multiplied the numerator and the denominator by the same number

Adding algebra fractions is done using the same method as you use for numbers

$$\frac{45q + 12q}{10} = \frac{57q}{10}$$

We have to leave this looking apparently top heavy because we don't know the value of q.

You can use the same method when you are subtracting fractions.

- 39 -

Algebra

Brackets

Any term or sign directly outside the bracket multiplies **all** the terms inside the bracket. e.g. $3(x + 4) = 3x + 12$ and $-2x(y - x) = -2xy + 2x^2$

note the change in the sign

e.g. $x - (y + z) = x - y - z$
$3 - (a + 9) = 3 - a - 9$
$= -6 - a$

Make sure that you can do all of the following:

$3(x - 4y) - y(3x - y) = 3x - 12y - 3xy + y^2$

note the change of sign

$a^2 - a(b + a)$
$= a^2 - ab - a^2$
$= -ab$

Factorising

Don't worry! The tie's not real snake skin.

Factorising is rewriting an expression (such as an answer in the previous section) by going the other way and putting in the brackets.

Given $9x - 12y$ find the largest common factor of the two terms and write it outside the bracket. The other factor of the term is written inside the brackets.

$9x - 12y = 3(3x - 4y)$
$10a^2b + 25ab^2 = 5ab(2a + 5b)$
$2\pi r^2 + 2\pi rh = 2\pi r(r + h)$

Harder brackets

remember to multiply everything in the second bracket by everything in the first

$(x + 2)(x - 4)$
$= x^2 - 4x + 2x - 8$
$= x^2 - 2x - 8$

Squaring brackets

$(3p - 7)^2 = (3p - 7)(3p - 7)$
$= 9p^2 - 21p - 21p + 49$
$= 9p^2 - 42p + 49$

squaring means multiplying by itself

The last two answers are called quadratic expressions. They follow the pattern $ax^2 + bx + c$ (b and/or c might be 0 but there is always an x^2 term).

Difference of 2 squares

This is a particular type of quadratic you need to be able to recognise.

Expand $(x + 3)(x - 3)$
$= x^2 - 3x + 3x - 9$
$= x^2 - 9$ This result is the **difference of two square terms**.

Note that the terms match but the signs are different.

Factorising the difference of 2 squares

e.g. $x^2 - 25 = (x + 5)(x - 5)$

$\sqrt{x^2}$ $\sqrt{25}$

The brackets have opposite signs.

Always write quadratic expressions with the x^2 term first, the x term second and the number term last.

Factorising quadratics

1

Factorise $x^2 + 4x$

$x^2 + 4x = x(x+4)$

The number term here is 0.

No bracket is needed here.

Most quadratics factorise into 2 factors which need 2 sets of brackets.

2

Factorise $x^2 + 5x + 6$

$6 = 1 \times 6 \quad\quad 1 + 6 = 7$
or $2 \times 3 \quad\quad \mathbf{2 + 3 = 5}$

$x^2 + 5x + 6 = (x + 2)(x + 3)$

1. Write down all the factors of the last term.
2. If the last term is positive then add the factors to get the coefficient for x.
3. If the last term is negative subtract the factors to get the coefficient for x.
4. Insert the numbers in brackets and put in the signs.
5. Multiply out to check.

3

Factorise $x^2 - 8x + 7$

$-7 \times -1 = 7$ ← the last term
$-7 + -1 = -8$ ← the middle term coefficient

$x^2 - 8x + 7 = (x - 7)(x - 1)$

You will need to practice these because at least one question based on quadratics is certain to appear in your exam.

4

Factorise $x^2 + 3x - 10$

$-10 = 2 \times -5 \quad\quad 2 + (-5) = -3$
or $-2 \times 5 \quad\quad -2 + 5 = 3$ ✓
or 1×-10
or -1×10

$x^2 + 3x - 10 = (x - 2)(x + 5)$

Two examples for you to practice with.

Factorise: **a.** $x^2 + 7x + 12$
b. $x^2 - 2x - 3$

The answers are given at the bottom of page 44.

Solving quadratic equations

$a \times b = 0$

Solve $x^2 + 3x - 10 = 0$
$\Rightarrow (x - 2)(x + 5) = 0$

$a \times b = 0$ means that either a or b or both must equal 0.

so either $(x - 2) = 0$ or $(x + 5) = 0$
$\Rightarrow x = 2$ or $x = -5$

check the answers by substituting into question line.
$2^2 + 3(2) - 10 = 0$ ✓
$-5^2 + 3(-5) - 10 = 0$ ✓

One side must = 0.
Rearrange if necessary.

$y = x^2 + 3x - 10$

The solutions are at points where the curve intersects with $y = 0$

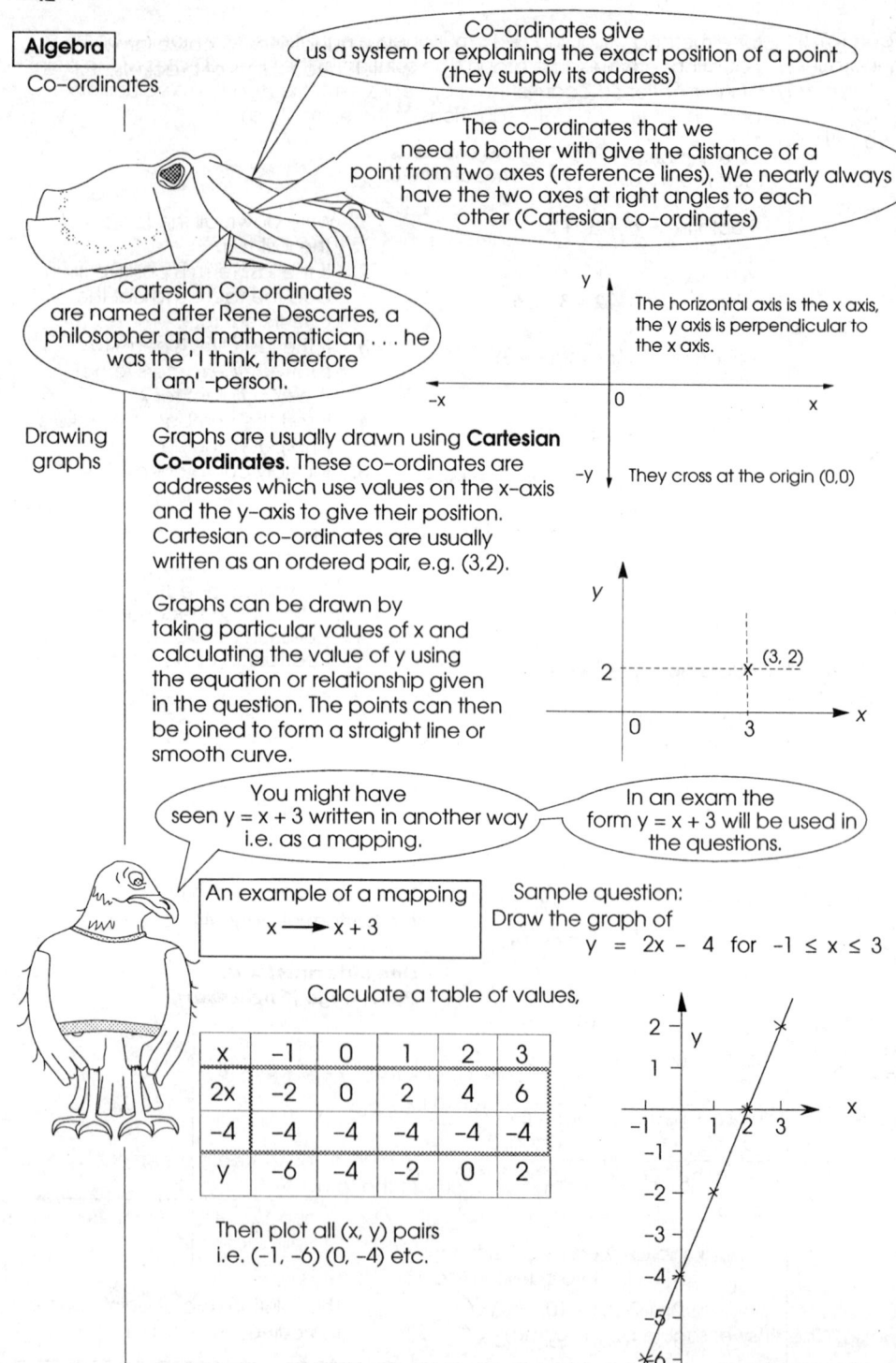

Algebra
Co-ordinates

Co-ordinates give us a system for explaining the exact position of a point (they supply its address)

The co-ordinates that we need to bother with give the distance of a point from two axes (reference lines). We nearly always have the two axes at right angles to each other (Cartesian co-ordinates)

Cartesian Co-ordinates are named after Rene Descartes, a philosopher and mathematician . . . he was the 'I think, therefore I am'-person.

The horizontal axis is the x axis, the y axis is perpendicular to the x axis.

They cross at the origin (0,0)

Drawing graphs

Graphs are usually drawn using **Cartesian Co-ordinates**. These co-ordinates are addresses which use values on the x-axis and the y-axis to give their position. Cartesian co-ordinates are usually written as an ordered pair, e.g. (3,2).

Graphs can be drawn by taking particular values of x and calculating the value of y using the equation or relationship given in the question. The points can then be joined to form a straight line or smooth curve.

You might have seen y = x + 3 written in another way i.e. as a mapping.

In an exam the form y = x + 3 will be used in the questions.

An example of a mapping
x ⟶ x + 3

Sample question:
Draw the graph of
$y = 2x - 4$ for $-1 \leq x \leq 3$

Calculate a table of values,

x	-1	0	1	2	3
2x	-2	0	2	4	6
-4	-4	-4	-4	-4	-4
y	-6	-4	-2	0	2

Then plot all (x, y) pairs
i.e. (-1, -6) (0, -4) etc.

Algebra

Solving simultaneous equations graphically

One method of solving two simultaneous equations is by plotting both equations on the same graph. The solution is the co-ordinates of the point of intersection. (Because the graphs have intersected these values of x and y must work in both equations at the same time).

$$y + 3x = 7 \quad \text{①}$$
$$x - y = 1 \quad \text{②}$$

Plot ① and ② as two straight lines on the same axes.
(see the previous page for one method)

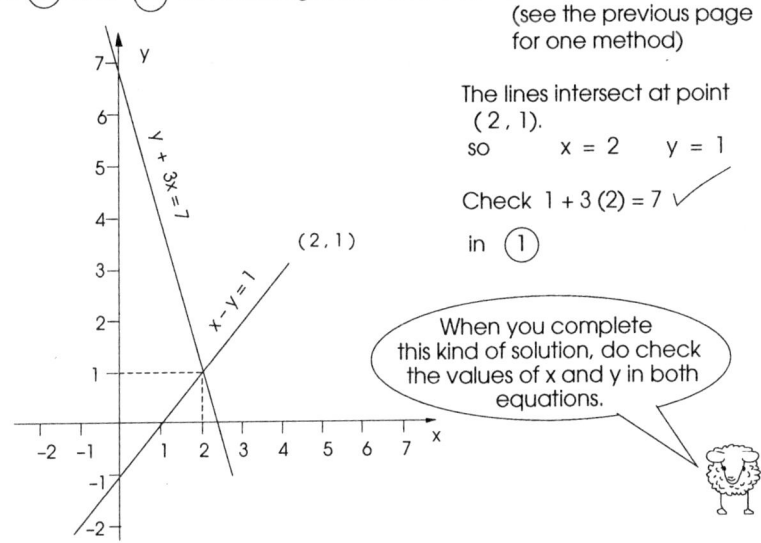

The lines intersect at point (2, 1).
so $x = 2 \quad y = 1$

Check $1 + 3(2) = 7$ ✓ in ①

When you complete this kind of solution, do check the values of x and y in both equations.

Solving simultaneous equations algebraically

Find the values of x and y which satisfy both these equations of straight lines. (This is the point (x,y) where the lines intersect.)

① $8x + 10y = -3$
② $11x - 10y = 60$

To get started, either the x terms or the y terms from each equation must match.

$19x = 57$

Add ① and ② because terms in 10y have different signs.

$$x = \frac{57}{19} = 3$$

To find the value of y, substitute $x = 3$ into equation ①

$24 + 10y = -3$
$10y = -27$
$y = -2 \cdot 7$

N.B. Check these answers by substituting into equation ②

Some times it may be necessary to multiply one or both equations by a constant before eliminating one of the terms.

① $7x + 2y = 19$
② $4x + 3y = 22$

Multiply ① by 3 and ② by 2 then subtract ② from ① to eliminate the y terms.
Now you finish.

Use this algebraic method to solve the two equations from the graphs at the top of the page. (The answer should be the same)

Answer:
$x = 1 \quad y = 6$

– 44 –

Algebra

a. Plot the graphs of $y = x^3 - 2x$ and $y = \frac{3}{x}$ for $-3 \leq x \geq 3$ on the same graph.

b. Find values of x where $x^3 - 2x = \frac{3}{x}$

Answer a.

Graphs of cubic and reciprocal functions

x	-3	-2	-1	0	1	2	3
x^3	-27	-8	-1	0	1	8	27
-2x	6	4	2	0	-2	-4	-6
y	-21	-4	1	0	-1	4	21

note the linear pattern

x	-3	-2	-1	0	1	2	3
$\frac{3}{x}$	-1	-1·5	-3	no value	3	1·5	1

these = y values

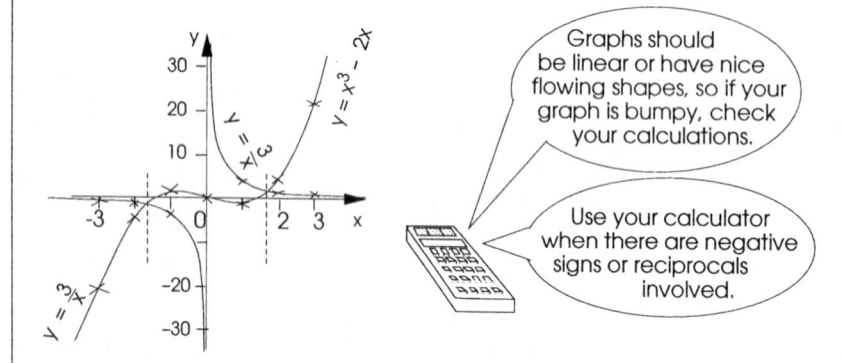

Graphs should be linear or have nice flowing shapes, so if your graph is bumpy, check your calculations.

Use your calculator when there are negative signs or reciprocals involved.

To find values of x where $x^3 - 2x = \frac{3}{x}$, you can read them from the graph by drawing verical lines from the points of intersection to the x axis.

Answer b. The answer to question **b.** is 1·75 or -1·75. This would be a reasonable level of accuracy from a graph with a scale of 1cm to 1 unit on the x axis.

> You should know what your graphs are likely to look like before you plot them. Do learn the basic shapes given in this algebra section.

Earning marks in an exam

1. Draw a single line passing through all the points exactly.
2. Use a sharp pencil— not crayon or felt tipped pens!

Answers (to the two questions on page 41)

$x^2 + 7x - 12 = (x + 3)(x + 4)$
$x^2 - 2x + 3 = (x - 3)(x + 1)$

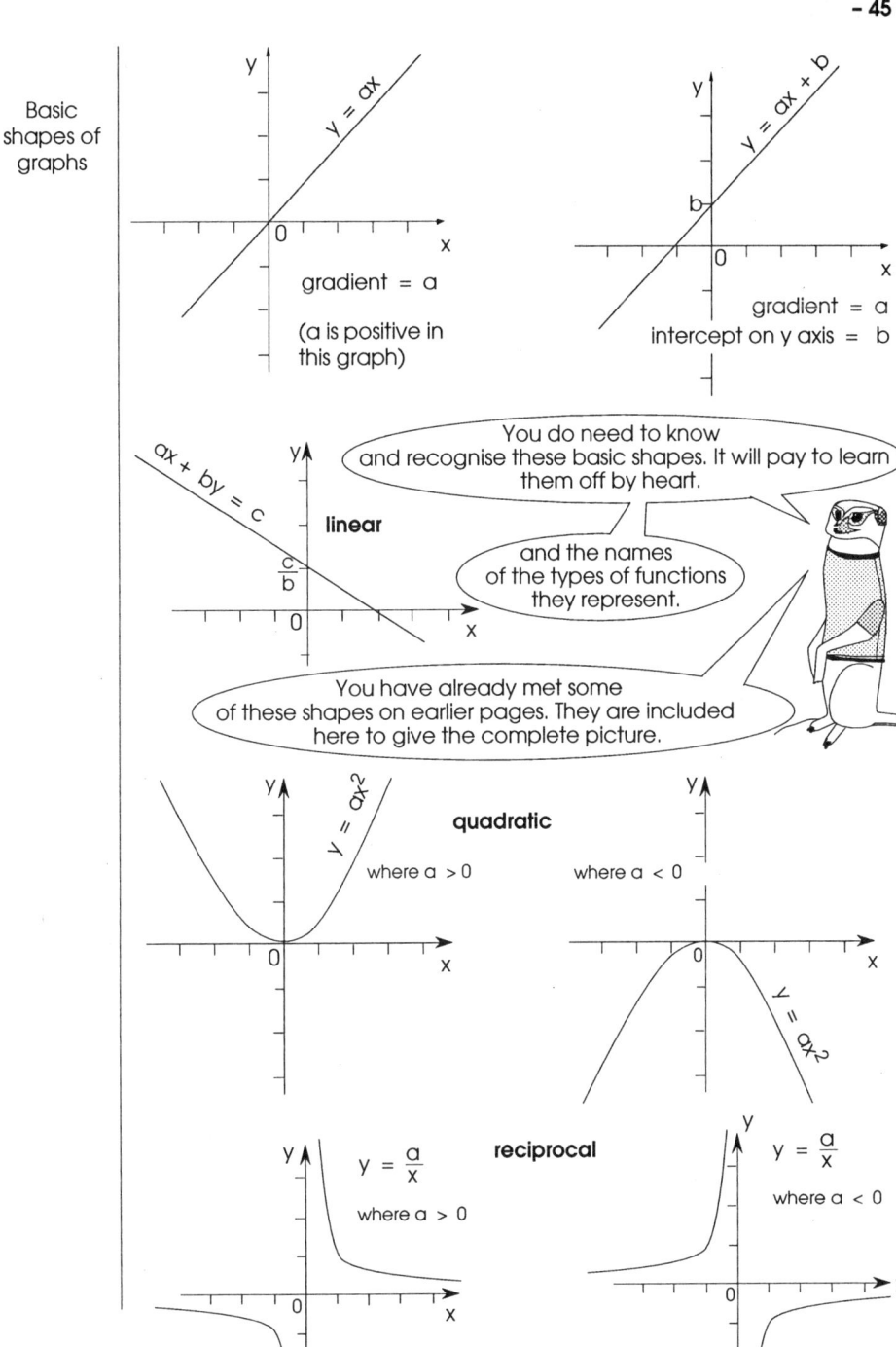

Basic shapes of graphs

$y = ax$

gradient = a

(a is positive in this graph)

$y = ax + b$

gradient = a
intercept on y axis = b

$ax + by = c$

linear

You do need to know and recognise these basic shapes. It will pay to learn them off by heart.

and the names of the types of functions they represent.

You have already met some of these shapes on earlier pages. They are included here to give the complete picture.

$y = ax^2$

quadratic

where a > 0

where a < 0

$y = ax^2$

reciprocal

$y = \dfrac{a}{x}$

where a > 0

$y = \dfrac{a}{x}$

where a < 0

Algebra

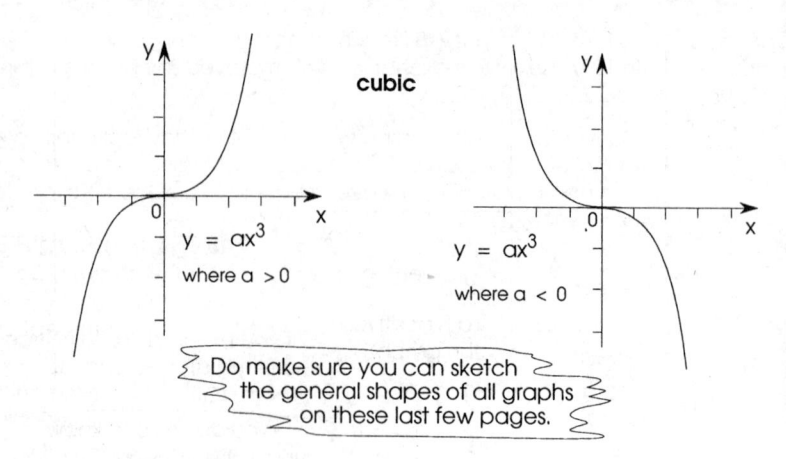

cubic

$y = ax^3$
where $a > 0$

$y = ax^3$
where $a < 0$

Do make sure you can sketch the general shapes of all graphs on these last few pages.

Many real life happenings can be graphed as a function of time; sporting events, temperature, radioactive decay, concentration of medicine in the bloodstream, weight loss.

If you are asked to interpret a graph, the ideas have probably been borrowed from science. Imagine your problem in a practical world and it might be easier to answer.

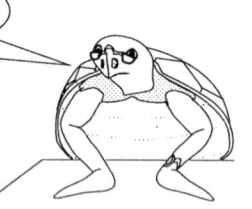

Travel graphs

This is a graph of a hill walker's journey.
(It does not represent the outline of the hill !)

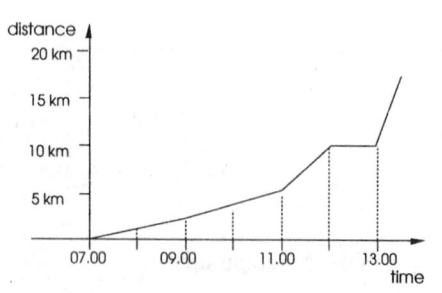

a. When was she 10 km from the start ?

b. How far had she gone by 13.00 hrs ?

The gradients in this case give the average speed over each hour. I think she borrowed a bike at 13.00 hrs after she had a rest.

Answers:
a. 12•00
b. 10 km
(he rested from 12•00 to 13•00)

- 47 -

Conversion graphs

In 1996 £1 bought 7·5 French Francs.
In 1997 the rate of exchange had improved (for people buying Francs) and £1 bought 10F.Fr.

Conversion graphs can be used as quick ready-reckoners to give a rough idea of how much money you get in another currency. Anybody can multiply by 10 and so we are going to use the 1996 rate for our conversion graph.

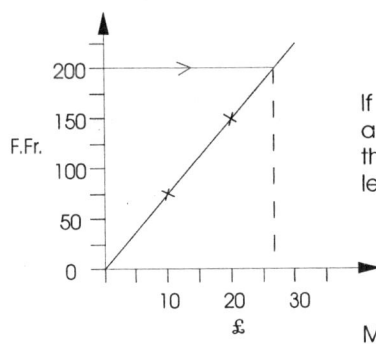

The gradient re F.Fr. per £ is the rate of exchange i.e. 7·5 F.Fr. / £.

If you bring back 200 F.Fr. and sell them to a friend at the same rate you bought them at, the dotted line on the graph will lead to your cash i.e. roughly £27.

Scales often have to be different on conversion graphs.

My calculation of 200 ÷ 7·5 = £ 26·67 needs a calculator or long division.

Rates of change

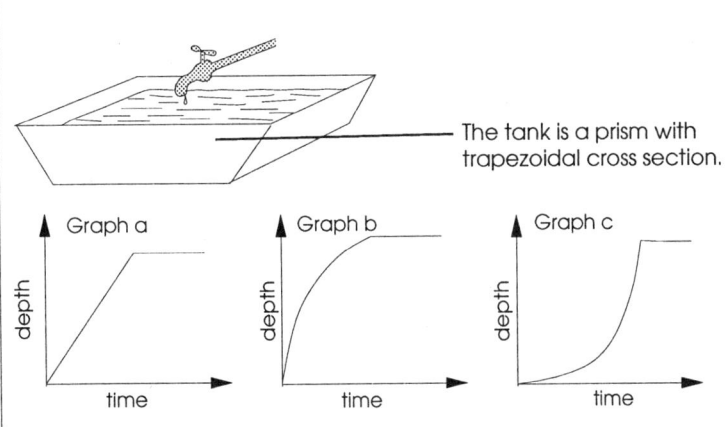

The tank is a prism with trapezoidal cross section.

Graph a   Graph b   Graph c

The water is flowing into the tank at a steady rate and one of the three graphs shows what is happening correctly.
   a. Which graph represents the changing depth of the water ?
      (Give a reason for your answer).
   b. What does the horizontal part of the curve represent ?

Answers:
 a. Graph b correctly shows what is happening.
    Reason: As the tank widens, the depth increases more slowly.
 b. When the tank is full the depth does not increase further.

– 48 –

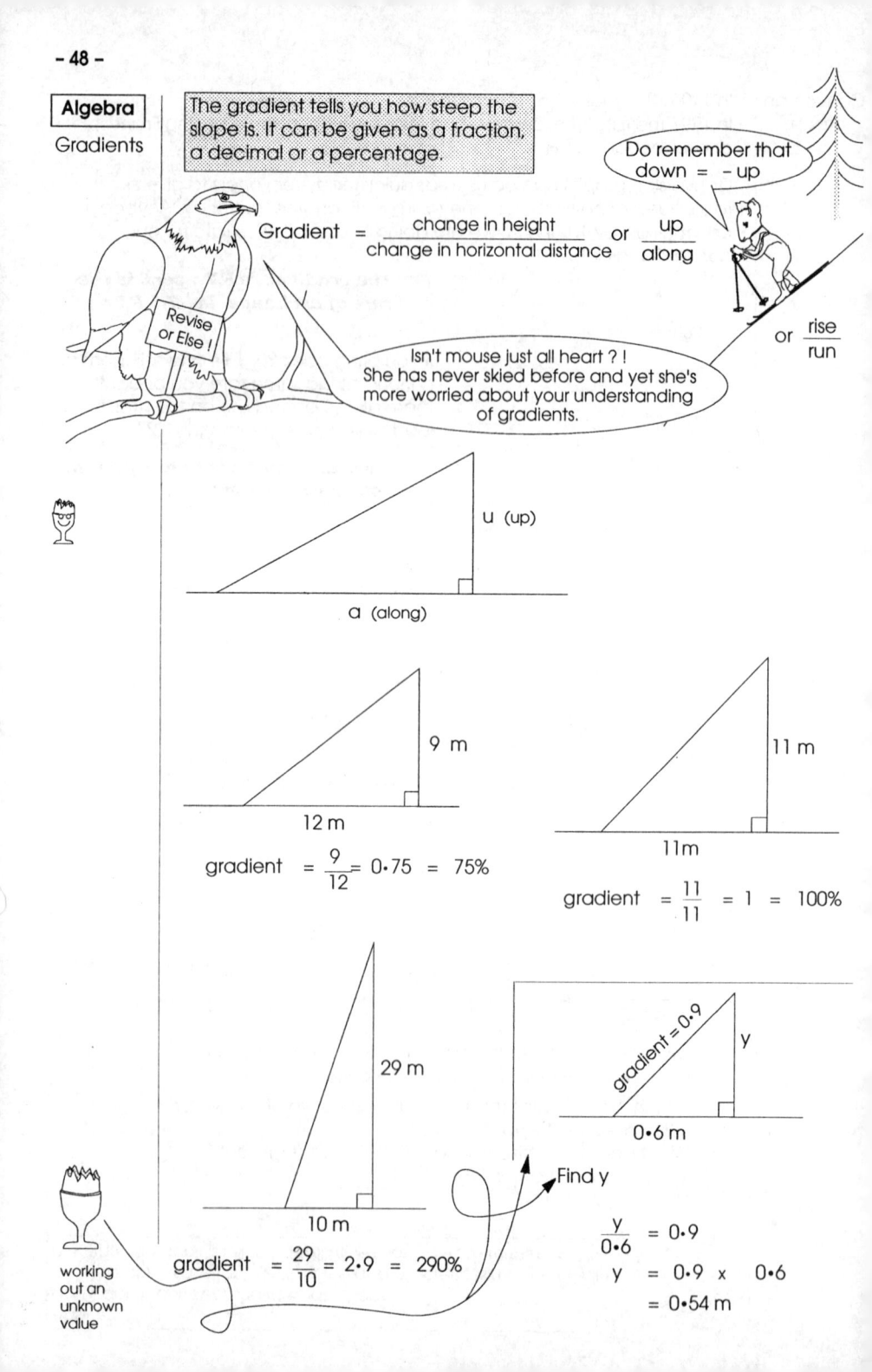

Algebra
Gradients

The gradient tells you how steep the slope is. It can be given as a fraction, a decimal or a percentage.

Do remember that down = –up

$$\text{Gradient} = \frac{\text{change in height}}{\text{change in horizontal distance}} \quad \text{or} \quad \frac{\text{up}}{\text{along}} \quad \text{or} \quad \frac{\text{rise}}{\text{run}}$$

Revise or Else!

Isn't mouse just all heart?! She has never skied before and yet she's more worried about your understanding of gradients.

u (up)
a (along)

9 m, 12 m

gradient = $\frac{9}{12}$ = 0·75 = 75%

11 m, 11 m

gradient = $\frac{11}{11}$ = 1 = 100%

29 m, 10 m

gradient = $\frac{29}{10}$ = 2·9 = 290%

gradient = 0·9, y, 0·6 m

Find y

$\frac{y}{0·6}$ = 0·9

y = 0·9 × 0·6
  = 0·54 m

working out an unknown value

Straight line or linear functions

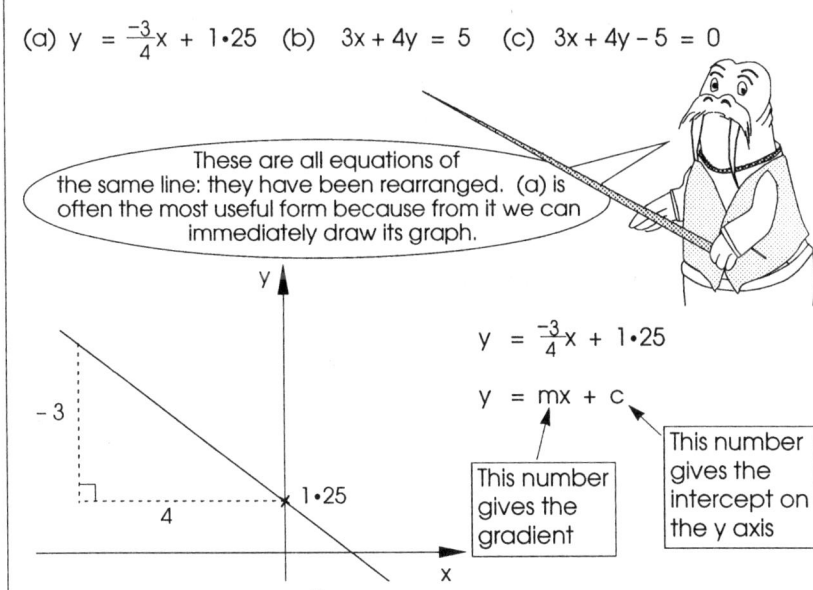

(a) $y = \frac{-3}{4}x + 1\cdot 25$ (b) $3x + 4y = 5$ (c) $3x + 4y - 5 = 0$

These are all equations of the same line: they have been rearranged. (a) is often the most useful form because from it we can immediately draw its graph.

$y = \frac{-3}{4}x + 1\cdot 25$

$y = mx + c$

This number gives the gradient

This number gives the intercept on the y axis

Proportionality   If q is connected to p^2 it might be better to draw the graph of (p^2, q). This would give a straight line.
The equation describing it would be:
$q = ap^2 + b$ here a is the gradient and b is the intercept on the y axis.
This method is particularly useful if the values are observed physical quantities, and you want to work out the connection/relationship between them.

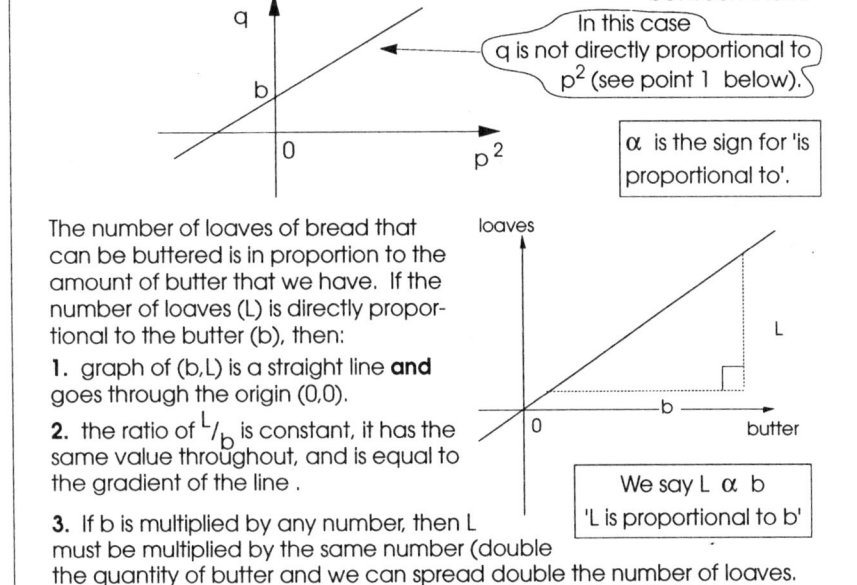

In this case q is not directly proportional to p^2 (see point 1 below).

α is the sign for 'is proportional to'.

The number of loaves of bread that can be buttered is in proportion to the amount of butter that we have. If the number of loaves (L) is directly proportional to the butter (b), then:
1. graph of (b,L) is a straight line **and** goes through the origin (0,0).
2. the ratio of $^L/_b$ is constant, it has the same value throughout, and is equal to the gradient of the line.
3. If b is multiplied by any number, then L must be multiplied by the same number (double the quantity of butter and we can spread double the number of loaves.

We say L α b
'L is proportional to b'

| Algebra |

Testing for proportionality

How can you test a table of values to see if one of the quantities is directly proportional to the other? (use fact 3 from above).

x 1·083 →

x	1·3	3·9	7·8	11·7
y	1·2	3·6	7·2	10·8

x ?

or use fact 1: Plot pairs of corresponding values on a graph and check that the line is straight and that it passes through the origin (0,0).

Experiments often leave us with loads of numerical results. These can be plotted on a graph. We then have a 'picture' that we can check for proportionality.

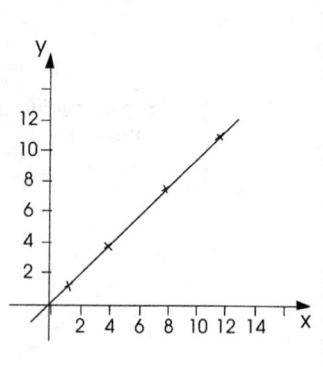

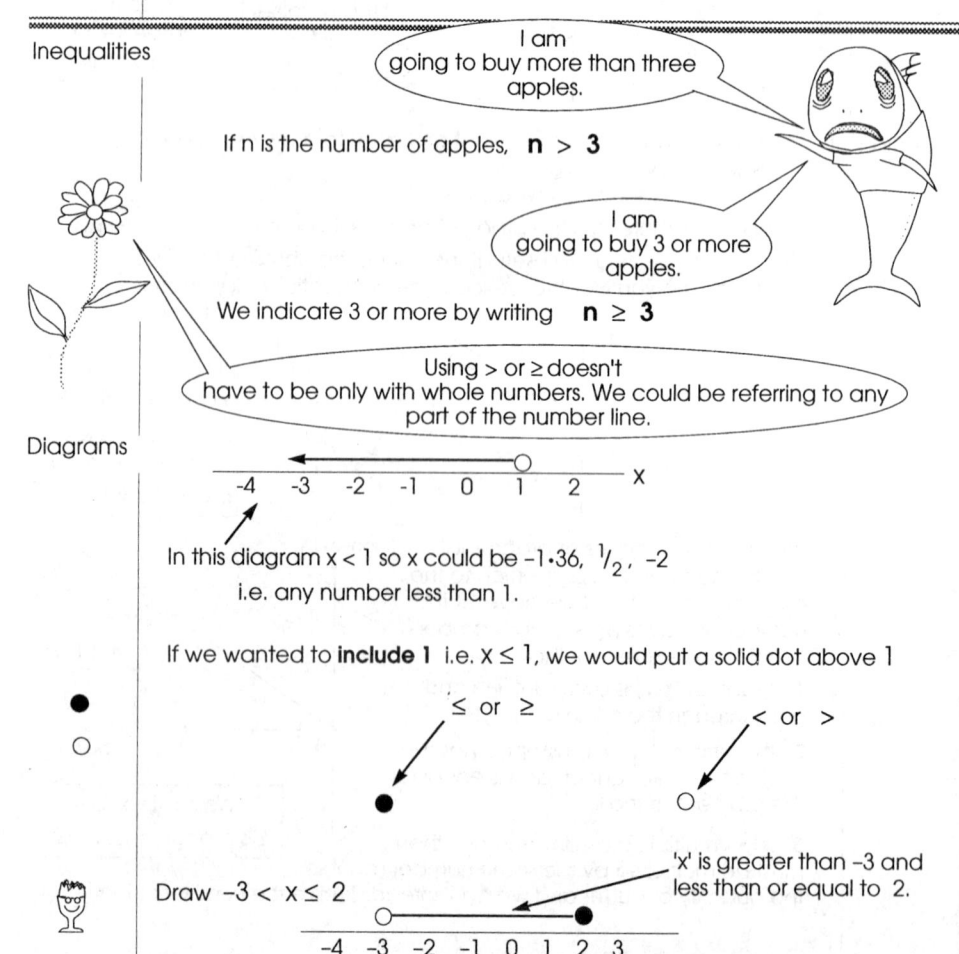

Inequalities

I am going to buy more than three apples.

If n is the number of apples, **n > 3**

I am going to buy 3 or more apples.

We indicate 3 or more by writing **n ≥ 3**

Using > or ≥ doesn't have to be only with whole numbers. We could be referring to any part of the number line.

Diagrams

-4 -3 -2 -1 0 1 2   x

In this diagram x < 1 so x could be -1·36, $1/2$, -2
i.e. any number less than 1.

If we wanted to **include** 1 i.e. x ≤ 1, we would put a solid dot above 1

≤ or ≥   < or >

Draw −3 < x ≤ 2

-4 -3 -2 -1 0 1 2 3

'x' is greater than −3 and less than or equal to 2.

Solving simple inequalities

When solving inequalities, we use the same method as for solving equations but when dividing or multiplying by a **negative** number, reverse the inequality sign.

1.
$$3x + 9 > 16 \quad \text{subtract 9 from both sides}$$
$$3x + 9 - 9 > 16 - 9$$
$$3x > 7 \quad \text{now multiply by } \tfrac{1}{3} \text{ (or } \div \text{ by 3)}$$
$$\tfrac{3x}{3} > \tfrac{7}{3}$$
$$\text{so } x > 2\tfrac{1}{3} \text{ or } x > 2\cdot\dot{3}$$

Don't round off in this type of problem...

2.
$$2 - 5x < \tfrac{1}{2}x$$
$$\Rightarrow 2(2 - 5x) < 2 \times \tfrac{1}{2}x$$
$$\Rightarrow 4 - 10x < x \quad \text{now +10x to both sides}$$
$$4 < 11x$$
$$\tfrac{4}{11} < x$$

Because the question has vulgar fractions it is better to leave the answer that way.

Forming inequalities

I have 3 boxes of chocolates and 14 single chocolates.
I have more chocolates than my friend who has 4 boxes of chocolates and 2 single chocolates.
Write down an inequality with x = number of chocs in a box.

Answer: $3x + 14 > 4x + 2$ ***never be tempted to use an = sign.***
$\qquad\quad 14 > x + 2$ ***You may forget to change it back***
$\qquad\quad 12 > x$ ***at the end.***

Check your answer by choosing a number in this range e.g. x is 5.
Substitute. $3(5) + 14 > 4(5) + 2$
$\qquad\qquad\quad 29 > 22 \checkmark$

If you multiply or divide by a negative number you must reverse the inequality sign.

$$\tfrac{7}{2} > 12 - 10x$$
$$\quad\text{multiply by 2}$$
$$2 \times \tfrac{7}{2} > 2(12 - 10x)$$
$$7 > 24 - 20x \quad \text{subtract 24}$$
$$-17 > -20x$$
$$\tfrac{17}{20} < x$$

Note that the inequality sign has reversed.

Algebra

Often the answer can be seen at a glance but it is better not to take chances. Draw sketch graphs whenever x^2 is involved.

Solve $x^2 \geq 16$

any value in this range marked:

◄—● and ●—►

gives $x^2 \geq 16$

so $x \leq -4$ and $x \geq 4$

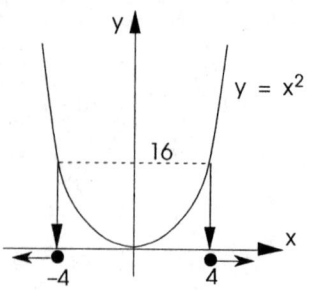

Find the values of x which satisfy:
$x^2 - 7 < 42$

The answer is at the bottom of the page

Regions

A graph represents the points which follow a particular rule
e.g. $x + y = 7$. For all points on the line the value of $x + y$ is equal to 7

So on one side of the line the values $x + y$ must be **less** than 7, and on the other side of the line the values of $x + y$ must be **more** than 7.
To find out which is which, choose a point, substitute its co-ordinates into the equation, and compare the answer with 7, then label each region.

Find the region $2x + 3y \leq 10$
First, draw the line $2x + 3y = 10$
Then choose any point, e.g. (3,4). Substitute
these values into $2x + 3y$
$= 2(3) + 3(4)$
$= 6 + 12$
$= 18$

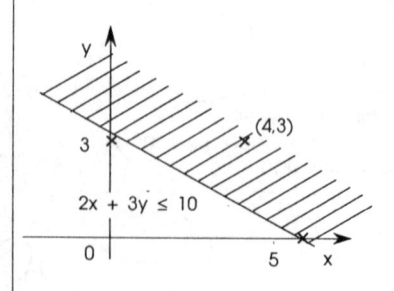

This is more than 10 so we want the other side of the line.

We have shaded the part that we don't want. Do read the question carefully to see which area to shade.

Ans. $-7 < x < 7$

- 53 -

Closed regions

Define the shaded triangular region.

Write down the equations of boundaries.
(i) $x = 5$
(ii) $y = 1$
(iii) Using $y = mx + c$ (see page 49)
      $y = 2x + 1$

So the shaded region is defined by:
(i) $x \leq 5$
(ii) $y \geq 1$
(iii) $y \leq 2x + 1$

(5,11)

(i) To check, chose a point, say (2, 2) and substitute values into your conditions.

$2 \leq 5$ $2 \geq 1$ $2 \leq 4 + 1$

This is true for all conditions so your answer is probably correct.

? Draw axes from -2 to 4 and show the region defined by the inequalities: $x + y < 3$ $y > -2$ $x > -1$

Does (0, 0) lie in the region?

Remember to use a dashed line -------- for < and >.

Answer

Yes, (0, 0) does lie in the region. Check that you have shaded the correct region by substituting

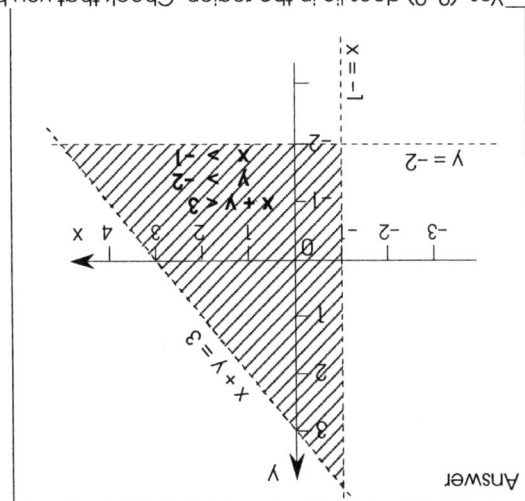

$0 + 0 < 3$
$0 > -2$
$0 > -1$

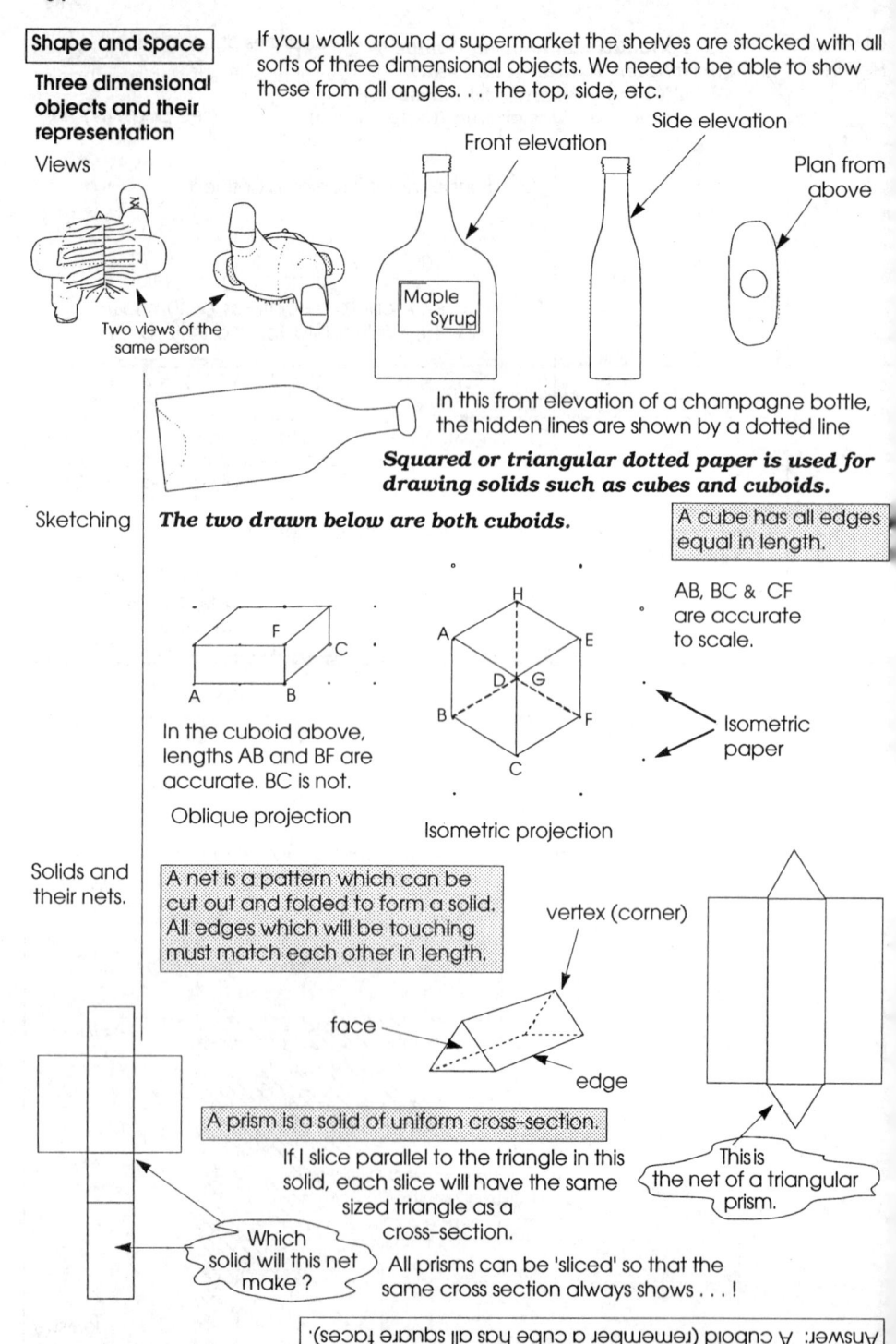

Shape and Space

Three dimensional objects and their representation

If you walk around a supermarket the shelves are stacked with all sorts of three dimensional objects. We need to be able to show these from all angles... the top, side, etc.

Views

Two views of the same person

Front elevation — Maple Syrup

Side elevation

Plan from above

In this front elevation of a champagne bottle, the hidden lines are shown by a dotted line

Squared or triangular dotted paper is used for drawing solids such as cubes and cuboids.

Sketching

The two drawn below are both cuboids.

> A cube has all edges equal in length.

In the cuboid above, lengths AB and BF are accurate. BC is not.

Oblique projection

AB, BC & CF are accurate to scale.

Isometric paper

Isometric projection

Solids and their nets

> A net is a pattern which can be cut out and folded to form a solid. All edges which will be touching must match each other in length.

vertex (corner)
face
edge

> A prism is a solid of uniform cross-section.

If I slice parallel to the triangle in this solid, each slice will have the same sized triangle as a cross-section.

This is the net of a triangular prism.

Which solid will this net make?

All prisms can be 'sliced' so that the same cross section always shows...!

Answer: A cuboid (remember a cube has all square faces).

A net for a square-based pyramid

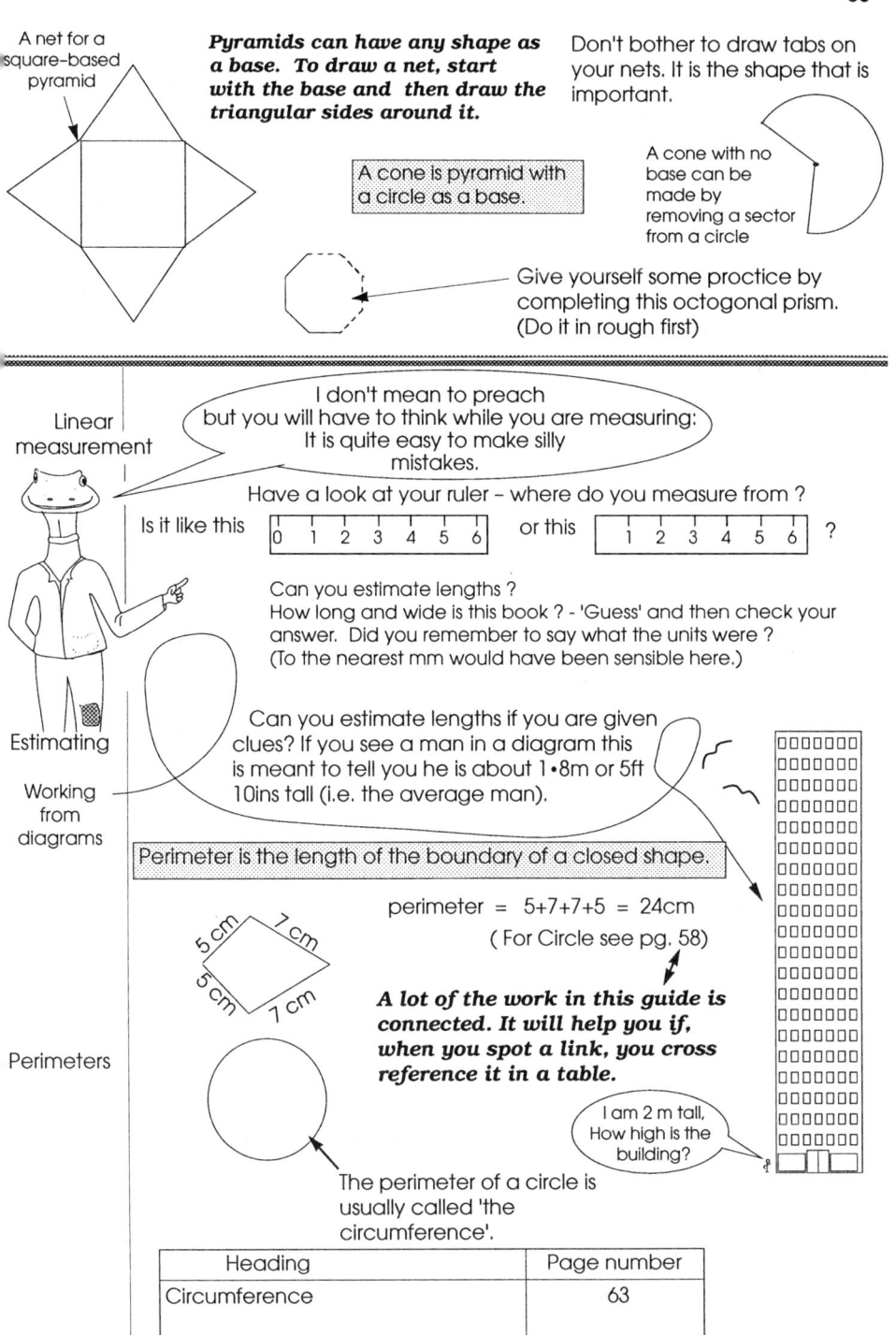

Pyramids can have any shape as a base. To draw a net, start with the base and then draw the triangular sides around it.

Don't bother to draw tabs on your nets. It is the shape that is important.

A cone is pyramid with a circle as a base.

A cone with no base can be made by removing a sector from a circle

Give yourself some practice by completing this octagonal prism. (Do it in rough first)

Linear measurement

I don't mean to preach but you will have to think while you are measuring: It is quite easy to make silly mistakes.

Have a look at your ruler – where do you measure from?

Is it like this | 0 1 2 3 4 5 6 | or this | 1 2 3 4 5 6 | ?

Can you estimate lengths?
How long and wide is this book? – 'Guess' and then check your answer. Did you remember to say what the units were?
(To the nearest mm would have been sensible here.)

Estimating

Working from diagrams

Can you estimate lengths if you are given clues? If you see a man in a diagram this is meant to tell you he is about 1·8m or 5ft 10ins tall (i.e. the average man).

Perimeter is the length of the boundary of a closed shape.

perimeter = 5+7+7+5 = 24cm
(For Circle see pg. 58)

A lot of the work in this guide is connected. It will help you if, when you spot a link, you cross reference it in a table.

Perimeters

I am 2 m tall, How high is the building?

The perimeter of a circle is usually called 'the circumference'.

Heading	Page number
Circumference	63

Shape and Space

Scale drawings

Scale drawings are diagrams of rooms, buildings etc..
They are exactly the same shape as the originals but are usually smaller.

If 1 cm on your diagram stands for 100 m and you have a field 220 m by 450 m, calculate the size of your diagram by :

$$\frac{220}{100} \text{cm} \times \frac{450}{100} \text{cm}$$

$$= 2.2 \text{ cm} \times 4.5 \text{ cm}.$$

sketch 220m
450m

220m
450m

Scale diagram drawn with ruler and sharp pencil.

Write real life measurements on your sketch and scale diagram.

An isosceles triangle has 2 sides 8 cm long and the equal angles are each 52°. Using a scale of 1cm to 2 cm to construct the triangle.

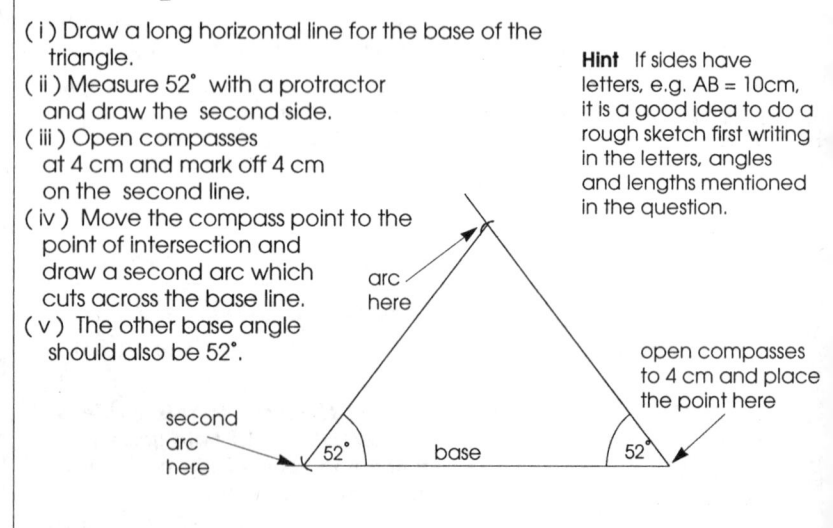

$$\frac{8}{2} = 4 \text{ cm}$$

(i) Draw a long horizontal line for the base of the triangle.
(ii) Measure 52° with a protractor and draw the second side.
(iii) Open compasses at 4 cm and mark off 4 cm on the second line.
(iv) Move the compass point to the point of intersection and draw a second arc which cuts across the base line.
(v) The other base angle should also be 52°.

Hint If sides have letters, e.g. AB = 10cm, it is a good idea to do a rough sketch first writing in the letters, angles and lengths mentioned in the question.

arc here

open compasses to 4 cm and place the point here

second arc here

52°   base   52°

Angles

Do have a care when you spell 'angle' Folks. Angels have wings, haloes and a lot of time on their hands.

Which shouldn't be true of all of us as we are so busy on revision!

Here are some facts about angles

A complete turn = 360°

A **right** angle = 90°
(a line at right angles to another is called **perpendicular**)

An **acute** angle is between 0° and 90°

A flat (**straight**) angle = 180°
(half a complete turn).

An **obtuse** angle is between 90° and 180°

A **reflex** angle is between 180° and 360°

Vertically opposite angles are equal.

What else do we need to know...?

Angles on a straight line add up to 180°.

• + ∝ + ○ = 180°

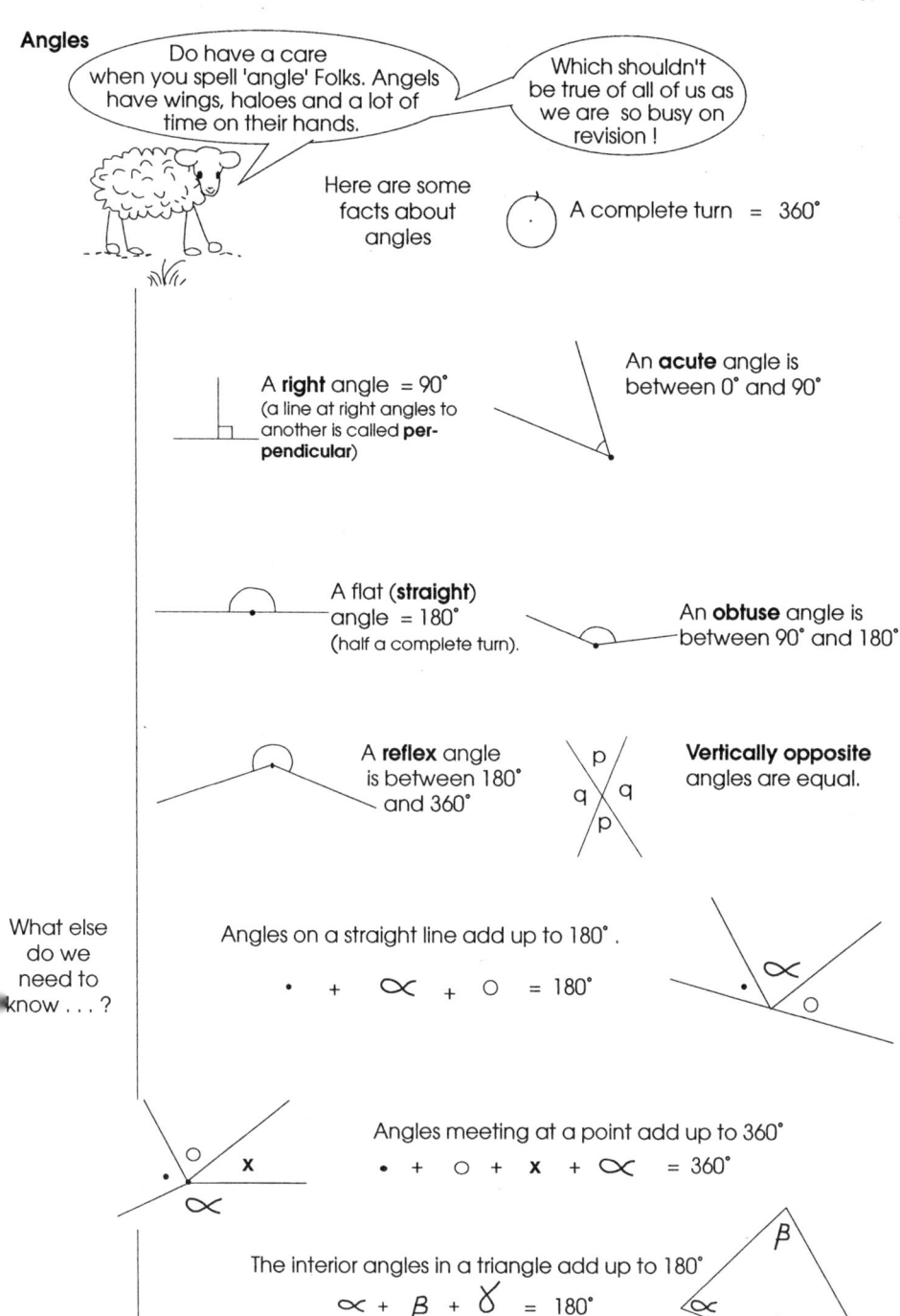

Angles meeting at a point add up to 360°

• + ○ + x + ∝ = 360°

The interior angles in a triangle add up to 180°

∝ + β + γ = 180°

- 57 -

| Shape and Space |

Exterior angle of a triangle

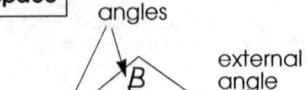

interior angles

external angle

$\alpha + \beta = 180 - \gamma$ — **Reason** Angles in a triangle
$\theta = 180 - \gamma$ — Angles on a straight line.
so $\theta = \alpha + \beta$

Exterior angle of a triangle = sum of opposite interior angles

Angles of a pentagon

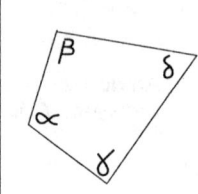

The interior angles in a **quadrilateral** add up to 360°

$\alpha + \beta + \delta + \gamma = 360°$

Find the interior angle of a regular polygon . . .
Cut the polygon (here it is a pentagon) into triangles from a single corner. Count the triangles and multiply by 180°

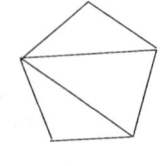

Sum of the interior angles = 3 x 180° = 540°
There are five sides to a pentagon, so there are five interior angles.

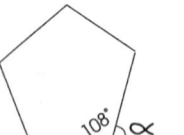

Each **interior** angle = $\dfrac{540°}{5}$ = 108°

The **exterior angle** = 180° - the interior angle
α = 180° - 108° = 72°

You can find sizes of angles in polygons by drawing the triangles (or learn the general result given at the bottom of the page).

Sum of interior angles of an n-sided polygon

There are 2 fewer triangles than sides so, if you have an n-sided polygon, there are (n - 2) triangles

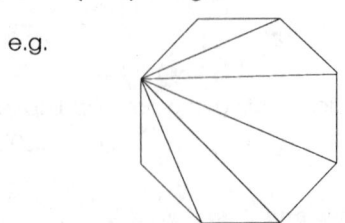

e.g.

8 sides, 6 triangles at 180° for each triangle.

Sum of the interior angles of a polygon = (n - 2) x 180°   180° = 2 x 90°
but (n - 2) x 180 = (n - 2) x 2 x (1 right angle)

sum = (2n - 4) right angles ◄——— This is worth learning.

A regular decagon has 10 sides.
Calculate:
    a. The sum of the interior angles.
    b. One interior angle.

a. Using the formula   sum = (2n − 4) right angles
                           = (2× 10 − 4) × 90
                           = 1440°
b. One angle = 1440 ÷ 10 = 144° ✓

Angles in parallel lines

Angles are formed when a line passes through parallel lines. It's worth knowing which of the angles are equal

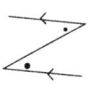

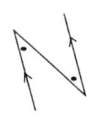

look for Z shapes

These **alternate** angles are equal.

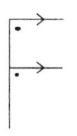

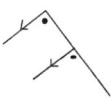

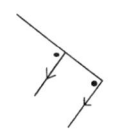

and F shapes

Angles in an F shape are **corresponding** and are equal.

Look for the Z or F shape, and decide which two angles are equal.

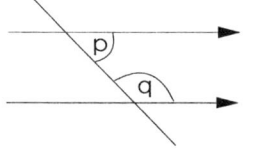

p + q = 180° p and q are **interior** angles.

Hint   *If you have parallel lines and 2 angles look the same, they probably are.*

If they look different sizes check if they add up to 180°.

Shape and Space

Measure bearings

Imagine you are facing North and only allowed to turn clockwise. P and Q are 2 towns. What is the bearing of Q from P?

Start by standing at P and **face North**. Turn **clockwise** until you face Q. Measure this angle with an angle measurer. (Estimate it first – it must be in between 0° and 90° in this case).

We usually use 3 figure bearings. For most angles this is straight forward but for acute angles, as in this example, we must add a 0 in front i.e. if the angle was 45°, the bearing would be 045° (read as zero four five degrees).

Plotting position

This angle is 360° – 220° = 140°

220°

Always draw North facing arrows at every location.

Town X is on a bearing of 220° at a distance of 4 km from V.
The scale of the map is
1 cm = 1 km
Or   1 : 100,000

Scales

Remember there are no units in this version because 100,000 cm = 1 km so we have a ratio.

North pointers are all parallel so it is then possible to use the properties of parallel lines to calculate other bearings such as:–

what is the bearing of V from X?

Bearing needed forms a set of interior angles with 140°.

x = 180° – 140°

Bearing of V from X is 040°

Plane shapes

I've always been a bit uneasy about 'plane', until now that is, but I've just looked at a definition and now don't know what all the fuss was about.

A plane is just a flat surface.

Parallel
Parallel lines are always the same distance apart – they will not meet no matter how long you extend them.

Descriptions of plane shapes

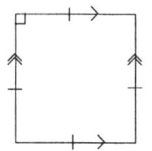

Square
All sides are equal.
Opposite sides are parallel
All angles are 90°
There are four lines of symmetry

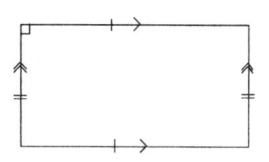

Rectangle
Opposite sides are equal
Opposite sides are parallel
All angles are 90°
There are two lines of symmetry

All 4 sided shapes are called quadrilaterals. The quadrilaterals with special properties have been included in this section.

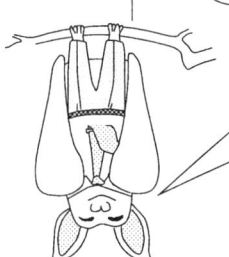

Please make sure that you can use these shapes to: **a** fit shapes together **b** recognise them in complicated diagrams

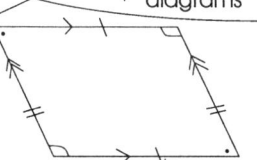

Parallelogram
Opposite sides are equal
Opposite sides are parallel
Opposite angles are equal
(Diagonals bisect each other)
Adjacent angles are supplementary (they add up to 180°)
There is rotational symmetry only

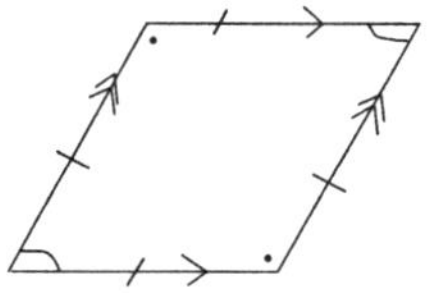

Rhombus
All sides are equal
Opposite sides are parallel
Opposite angles are equal
(Diagonals bisect each other at 90°)
Adjacent angles are supplementary (they add up to 180°)
There are two lines of symmetry

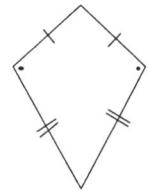

Kite
Two pairs of equal adjacent sides
One pair of opposite angles are equal
One line of symmetry

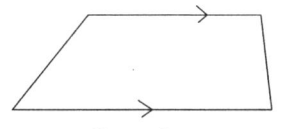

Trapezium
One pair of sides is parallel

Triangles

Triangle
A closed, three-sided shape, the interior angles add up to 180°

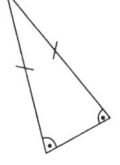

Isosceles triangle
Two sides are equal
The base angles are equal
1 line of symmetry

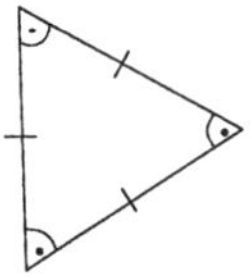

Equilateral triangle
all three sides are equal
3 angles are equal (60°)
3 lines of symmetry

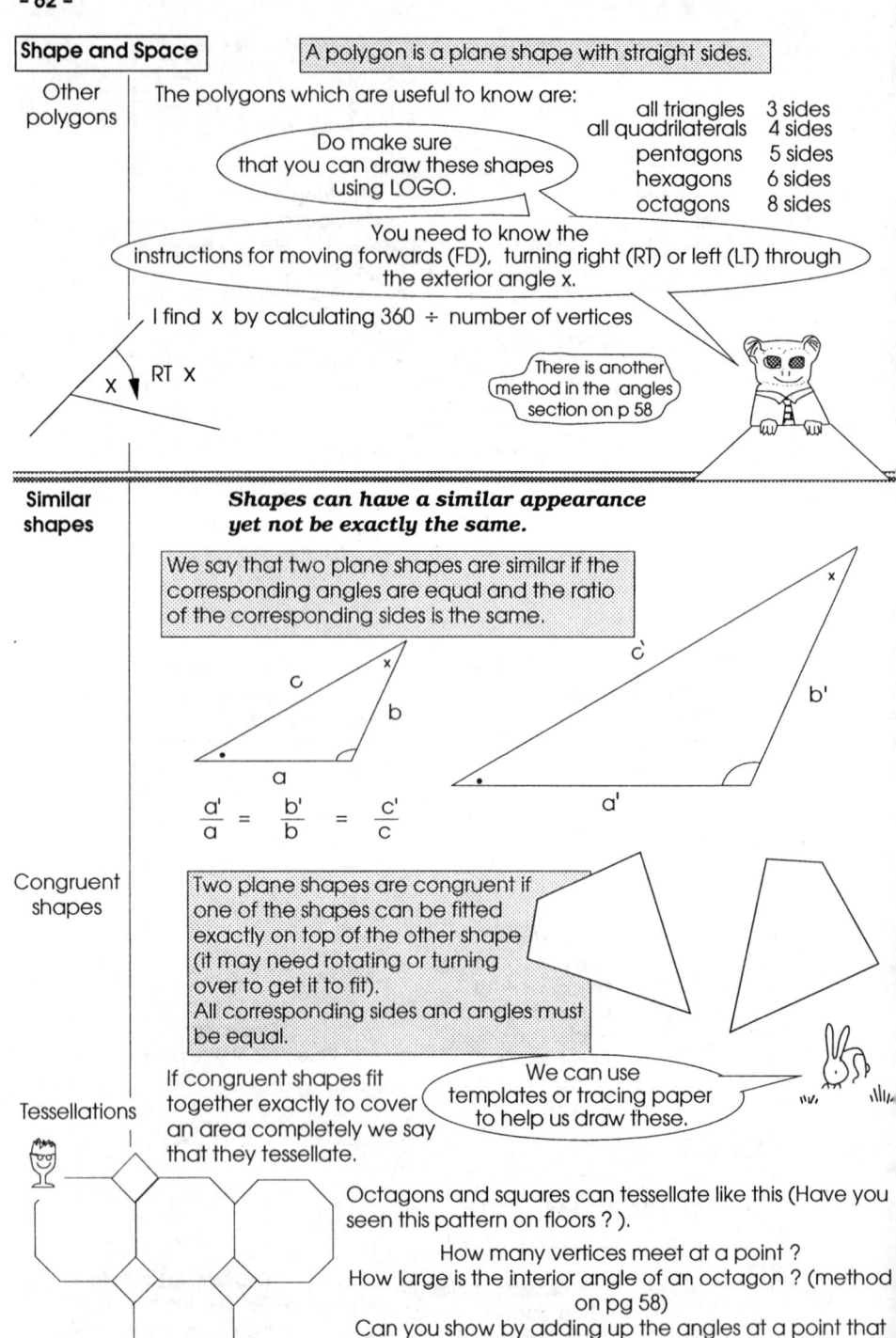

Shape and Space

A polygon is a plane shape with straight sides.

Other polygons

The polygons which are useful to know are:

all triangles	3 sides
all quadrilaterals	4 sides
pentagons	5 sides
hexagons	6 sides
octagons	8 sides

Do make sure that you can draw these shapes using LOGO.

You need to know the instructions for moving forwards (FD), turning right (RT) or left (LT) through the exterior angle x.

I find x by calculating 360 ÷ number of vertices

RT x

There is another method in the angles section on p 58

Similar shapes

Shapes can have a similar appearance yet not be exactly the same.

We say that two plane shapes are similar if the corresponding angles are equal and the ratio of the corresponding sides is the same.

$$\frac{a'}{a} = \frac{b'}{b} = \frac{c'}{c}$$

Congruent shapes

Two plane shapes are congruent if one of the shapes can be fitted exactly on top of the other shape (it may need rotating or turning over to get it to fit). All corresponding sides and angles must be equal.

Tessellations

If congruent shapes fit together exactly to cover an area completely we say that they tessellate.

We can use templates or tracing paper to help us draw these.

Octagons and squares can tessellate like this (Have you seen this pattern on floors?).

How many vertices meet at a point?
How large is the interior angle of an octagon? (method on pg 58)
Can you show by adding up the angles at a point that these shapes tessellate?

(continued)

To find the interior angle of an octagon use the formula:

$$\text{sum} = (2n - 4) \times 90$$
$$= (2 \times 8 - 4) \times 90 = 1080$$
$$\text{one angle} = \frac{1080}{8} = 135°$$

Angles at a point in the tessellation
= 135 + 135 + 90
= 360°   so they make a complete turn.

Circles

The **diameter** is the longest straight line you can draw across a circle. (It goes through the centre)

The line from the centre to the edge or perimeter (i.e. to the circumference) is called the **radius**.

2 x radius = diameter   r for radius
2r = d   d for diameter

Arc — An arc is part of the circumference.

Chord — A chord cuts the circle into two segments.

Tangent — A tangent is a straight line which touches a circle at a point, perpendicular to a radius.

Circumference — *We calculate the circumference by multiplying the diameter by the number π (pronounced 'pi').*

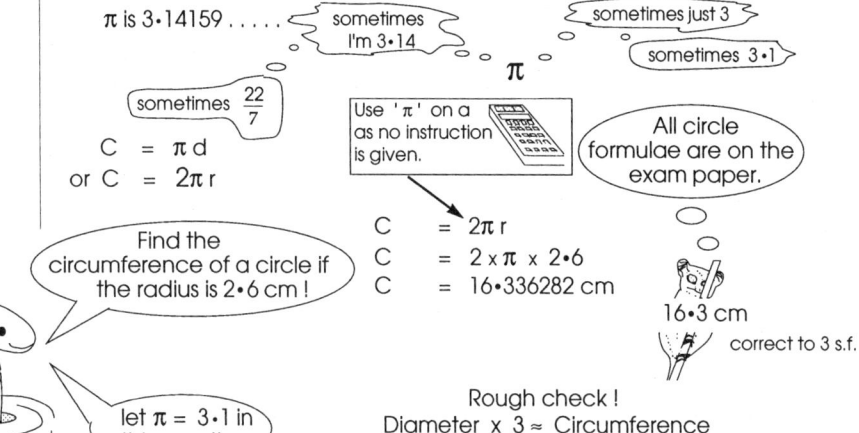

π is 3·14159 .....   sometimes I'm 3·14   sometimes just 3   sometimes 3·1

sometimes $\frac{22}{7}$

C = π d
or C = 2π r

Use 'π' on a as no instruction is given.

All circle formulae are on the exam paper.

Find the circumference of a circle if the radius is 2·6 cm !

C = 2π r
C = 2 x π x 2·6
C = 16·336282 cm

16·3 cm correct to 3 s.f.

let π = 3·1 in this question

Rough check !
Diameter x 3 ≈ Circumference

| Shape and Space | *The diameter is roughly one third of the circumference.* |

Finding the diameter

Find the diameter of a circle with C = 19•8 cm

$$C = \pi d \quad \text{so} \quad d = C \div \pi$$
$$d = 19•8 \div 3•1$$
$$d = 6•4 \text{ cm correct to 1 d. p.}$$

My bicycle wheel has a radius of 28 cm.

If my wheel goes round 1000 times how far have I travelled?

Hint: The circumference of the wheel touches the road.

How far in 1 revolution?

$$C = \pi d$$
$$C = \pi \times 28 \times 2$$
$$C = 175•92919 \text{ cm}$$

Keep this in the calculator.

Therefore in 1000 revolutions:

$$1000 \text{ revolutions} = 175•92919 \times 1000 \text{ cm}$$
$$= \frac{175•92919 \times 1000}{100} \text{ m}$$
$$= 1769 \text{ m or } 1•77 \text{ km to 3 s.f.}$$

÷ by 100 to get metres

≈ 1•77 km 3s.f.

Finding the area

The area of this shaded square is r x r i.e. r^2

so if we put 4 of them together, the total area will be 4 r^2

The area of this is $4r^2$

Obviously, the area of the circle that fits inside the square is less than $4r^2$. It is roughly $3r^2$; accurately, it is πr^2.

Area of a circle = πr^2

Find the area of a circle with radius 3•09 cm.

Let $\pi = 3•142$

$$A = \pi r^2$$
$$= 3•142 \times 3•09 \times 3•09$$
$$= 30•0$$

| 3•142 | x | 3•09 | x | 3•09 | = | 30•00013 |

note that the we have corrected the answer to 3 significant figures

= 30•0 cm to 3 sig. figs.

Finding a radius from the area

To calculate the area of a circle you follow the formula i.e. square the radius and multiply by π. ($A = \pi r^2$).
If you are given the area and are told to find the radius you must carry out the opposite or inverse steps i.e. divide by π, then find the square root.

If the area of a circle is 40·7 cm^2, find the radius.

$$r = \sqrt{\frac{40.7}{\pi}}$$

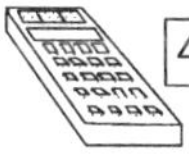

$\boxed{40\cdot7}\ \boxed{\div}\ \boxed{\pi}\ \boxed{=}\ \boxed{\sqrt{\ }}$ = 3·60 correct to 3 s. f.

or you could substitute in $A = \pi r^2$, rearrange and solve.

Circles and Angles

If you can find a right angled triangle in a problem you may be able to use either Pythagoras or Trigonometry to solve a question.

Try to spot all the right angles in the diagrams below.

Angles in a semi-circle

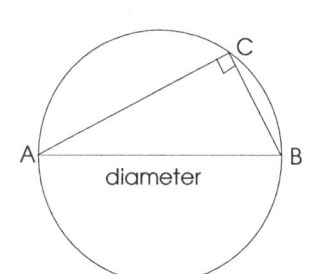

C can be anywhere on the circumference and $\hat{ACB}$ will always equal 90°.

*AB **subtends** $\hat{C}$ at the circumference.*

Perpendicular bisector of a chord

QP is a perpendicular bisector of chord XZ.
This means that $\hat{OYZ} = 90°$ and
$$XY = YZ$$
When these two facts are present there is a point O which is the centre of the circle i.e. OP is a radius.

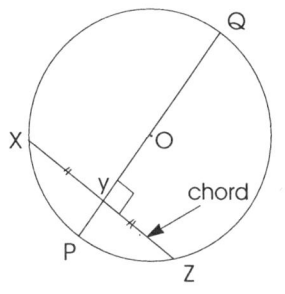

Angle between a radius and a tangent

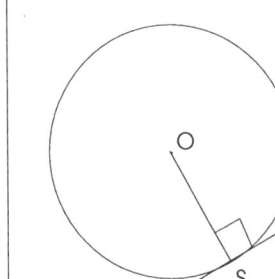

OST = 90°

When OS is a radius
RST is a tangent

A tangent is a straight line which touches a circle at a point.

Shape and Space

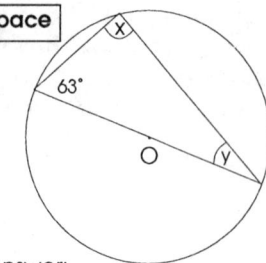

1. O is the centre of the circle. Find the angles marked x and y.

If the question asks you to 'find' or 'calculate',
do not measure with a ruler!
(you will score 0 marks)

Answer:
x is 90°   because it is subtended by a diameter.
y = 180 − (63 + 90)   Angles in a triangle add up to 180°
y = 27°

2. O is the centre of a circle.
QR = RS
Find OR̂S and OR

Answer:
OR̂S = 90°   OP is a radius and it bisects a chord so it must be perpendicular to the chord.

$\dfrac{OR}{10}$ = Cos 40   *see page for trogonometry*

⟹ OR = 10 × Cos 40   so OR = 7·66

Loci

A locus is just a word meaning all the points that fit a certain rule.

Sometimes the line or boundary is the part that matters, sometimes it is the area inside or beyond the boundary.

First draw the boundary/ locus that fits the description.

Draw it as a solid line if it is to be included in the area that is needed or as a dotted line if it is not

Please make sure that you can recognise and draw these 6 loci.

a. Locus of a point P at a given distance from a fixed point O.
OP = 1cm

We have used a solid line here.

Always leave all your construction lines on the paper when you draw loci. The examiner likes to see how you got your answer.

(Continued with further examples)

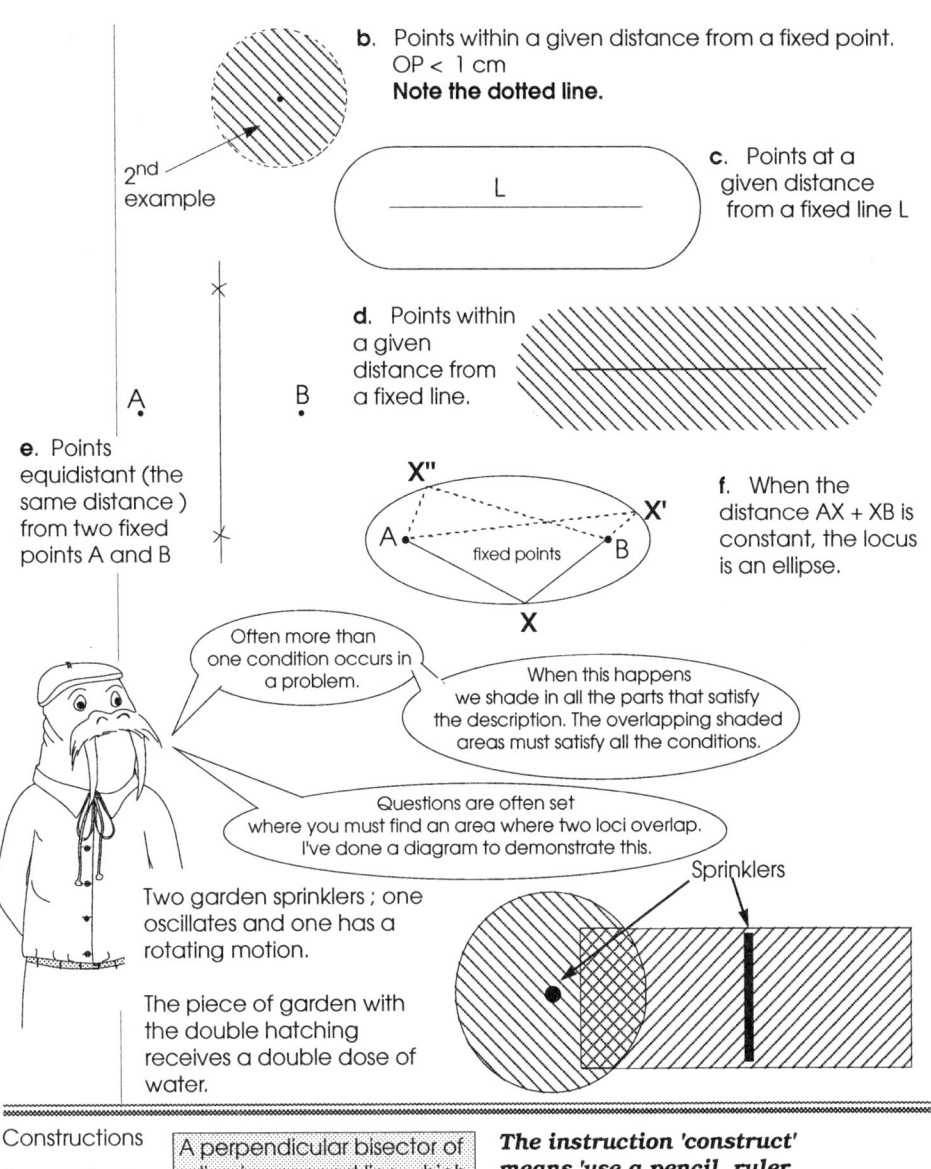

b. Points within a given distance from a fixed point.
OP < 1 cm
Note the dotted line.

2nd example

c. Points at a given distance from a fixed line L

d. Points within a given distance from a fixed line.

A

B

e. Points equidistant (the same distance) from two fixed points A and B

f. When the distance AX + XB is constant, the locus is an ellipse.

fixed points

Often more than one condition occurs in a problem.

When this happens we shade in all the parts that satisfy the description. The overlapping shaded areas must satisfy all the conditions.

Questions are often set where you must find an area where two loci overlap. I've done a diagram to demonstrate this.

Two garden sprinklers; one oscillates and one has a rotating motion.

Sprinklers

The piece of garden with the double hatching receives a double dose of water.

Constructions

Perpendicular bisector

A perpendicular bisector of a line is a second line which is at 90° **and** halves the line.

The instruction 'construct' means 'use a pencil, ruler and compasses'.

1. Draw the line that we need to bisect at the length given in the question.
2. Open your compasses until the gap is a bit longer than half the line.
3. Put the compass point on one end and make a long arc above and below the line.
4. Do the same on the other side.
5. Join up the points of intersection.

line 1

Shape and Space

Bisector of an angle

1. Draw the required angle.
2. Open your compasses until the gap is less than the shortest 'arm' of the angle (it might be part of a triangle).
3. Put the point on the vertex of the angle and draw arcs across both 'arms' of the angle.
4. Put the point on the intersection of arc and arm and draw another arc inside the angle.
5. Do the same on the other side.
6. Join the vertex to the intersection of the arcs.

'arm', first arcs, vertex

Construction of a 60° angle

When you see 60° think of equilateral triangles.

1. Draw a line.
2. Open compasses to the same length as the line.
3. Put the point on the end of the line and draw an arc on one side.
4. Do the same from the other end of the line.
5. Join one end to the the intersection.

You can construct a 90° angle and a perpendicular from a point to a line by using the ideas for constructing a perpendicular bisector.

60°

Metric and Imperial measures

People measure and estimate all the time in science, cooking, putting oil in the car or decorating the house. They use common sense to decide how accurate they need to be.

Measuring

There are no rules we can give you about levels of accuracy – just imagine the real life situation

Example 1. When buying a carpet: you would round **up** to the **nearest** 10 cm if your room measured 3·47m by 4·13 m you would buy 3·5m by 4·2m.

Example 2. When cooking a cake: Many scales still use ounces (oz) so you would measure to the nearest oz. i.e. the 8 oz of sugar might be from 7·5 to 8·5 oz. but that wouldn't really make much difference to the end result.

Reading from a scale

3 lb, 2 lb, 1 lb

1. Decide which way the numbers are getting larger.
2. Decide how the scale is divided i.e. what each mark or graduation represents.
3. Look at the position of the pointer and read the value.

2 litres, 1·6 litres, 1 litre

This scale reads $1\frac{3}{4}$ lbs or 1 lb 12 oz

$\left(\frac{3}{4} \times 16 = 12\right)$

You will be given the Imperial conversion factors in an exam question.

1·6l = 11 600 ml
(1000 ml = 1 litre)

But you are expected to know the metric conversion factors.

Conversions	Approximate conversions	More exact conversions
	8 km ≈ 5 miles	1 kg ≈ 2·2 lb
	1 litre ≈ $1\tfrac{3}{4}$ pints	1 m ≈ 39·37 in
		1 inch ≈ 2·54 cm
		1 ft ≈ 30·5 cm

Best to learn these off by heart.

Time

Time		
60 sec	=	1 min
60 min	=	1 hr
24 hrs	=	1 day
7 days	=	1 week
52 weeks	=	1 year
365 days	=	1 year
(366 in a leap year)		

30 days hath September, April, June and November. All the rest have 31, except February alone which has 28 days clear and 29 in each leap year.

Metric measurements

Remember
1 km = 1000 m
100 centimetres = 1 metre
10 millimetres = 1 centimetre
1000 grammes = 1 kg
1000 millilitres = 1 litre

Approximations:
finger tips of outstretched hand to opposite shoulder ≈ 1 m
Tip of the little finger ≈ 1 cm

It is important to realise that the digits never change during metric conversions, only the position of the decimal point.

1000 cc = **1000 cm³ = 1 litre**

I travel at 72 miles per hour.
What is this in km per hour?

$$72 \div 5 \times 8 \quad \text{or} \quad 72 \times \frac{8}{5} = 115 \cdot 2 \text{ km per hour}$$

logical approach:
I want a larger answer because kilometres are shorter than miles

Scale factor approach:
$$\frac{\text{going to km}}{\text{coming from miles}}$$

Pythagoras' rule

$$a^2 + b^2 = c^2$$

The Pythagoras chappy's rule applies only to right angled triangles.

The longest side will always be the hypotenuse (the side opposite the right angle). Use Pythagoras' rule when you are given the lengths of two sides of the triangle, and you have to calculate the third.

I don't mean to boss you Folks, but when solving these questions, always write down the formula first.

(continued)

$$a^2 + b^2 = c^2$$

Shape and Space

Pythagoras' rule

ABC is an isoceles triangle.
I want to find the area.

$A = \frac{1}{2} \times base \times height$

So I need to find the height ; lets call the bottom of the perpendicular ' X '.

We need to calculate XB :

$AB^2 = AX^2 + XB^2$
$8^2 = 3^2 + XB^2$ (AX is half AC)
$64 = 9 + XB^2$
$64 - 9 = XB^2$
$\sqrt{55} = XB$

Leave this in your calculator. Don't round off because you are going to carry it into the next calculation.

$7 \cdot 4161985 = XB$

Area A B C $= \frac{1}{2} \times 6 \times 7 \cdot 4161985 = 22 \cdot 2$ cm^2 to 3 sig. figs.

You must draw a diagram of this, and then fill in horizontal and vertical lengths.

P (–4, –3)
Q (4, –1)

Find the distance PQ.

Horizontal distance: $4 - (-4) = 8$

Vertical distance: $-1 - (-3) = 2$

$PQ^2 = 8^2 + 2^2$
$PQ^2 = 64 + 4$
$PQ = \sqrt{68}$
$PQ = 8 \cdot 25$ units (3 sig. fig.)

Areas

When we find areas we are finding out how much surface there is.

We use squares as the units (but not always)!

These two shapes both cover the same area i.e. 4 triangles.

There are several ways to find the shaded area :

6 m
5 m
3 m

(Continued)

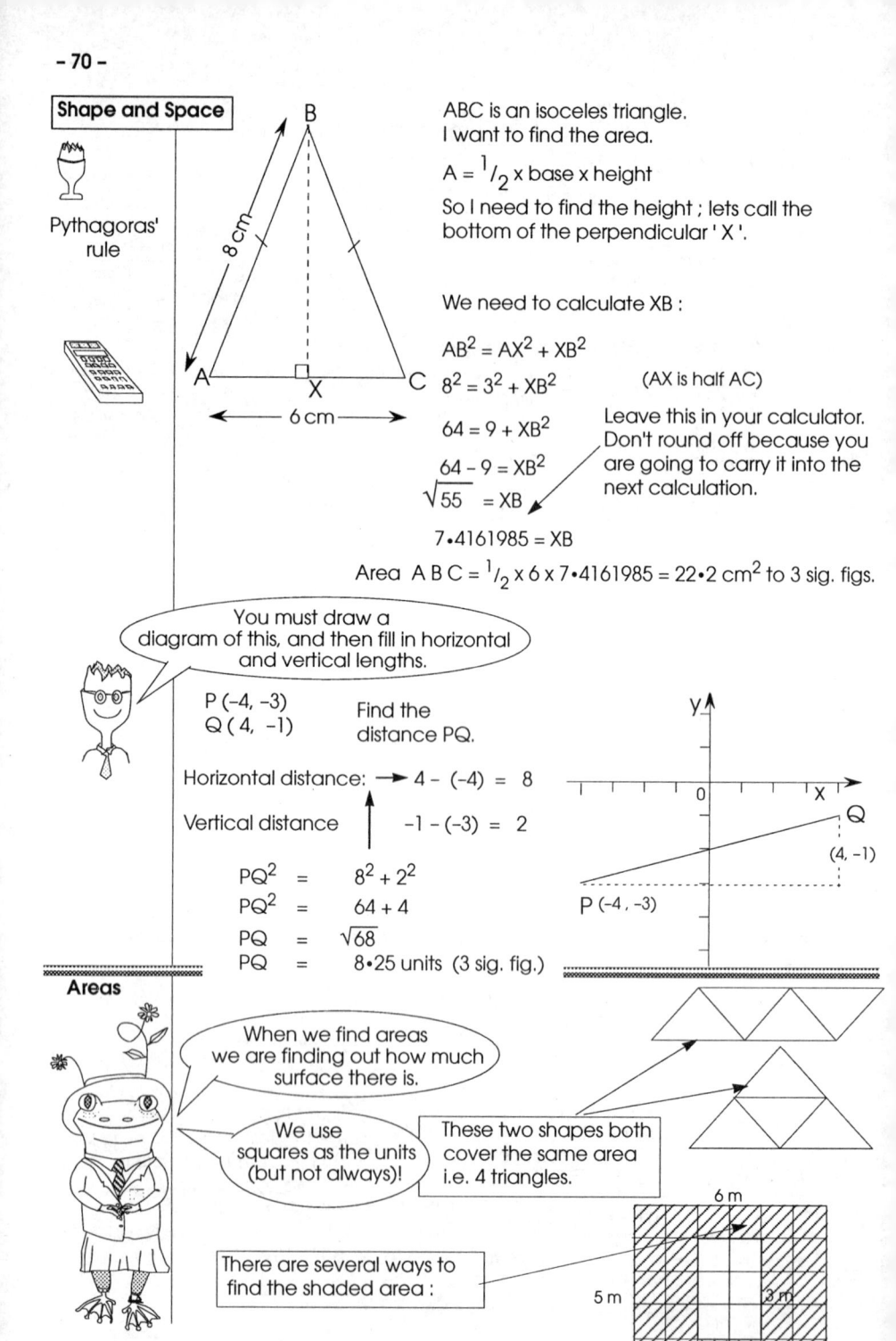

Estimating or measuring on a grid

1. Counting the squares gives the area as 24 m².

2. Calculate the areas of the large rectangle and the rectangle cut out of the middle and subtract.

$$6m \times 5m = 30m^2$$
$$2m \times 3m = \underline{6m^2}$$
$$24m^2$$

I get 20 squares. I'm not a giant frog, I'm just not drawn to scale.

Estimating the area of irregular shapes

To get the surface area of this luxury swimming pool, we can cover the outline with a grid of a scale we know (here each square is 4 m² and then count any squares that are more than half covered by the pool).

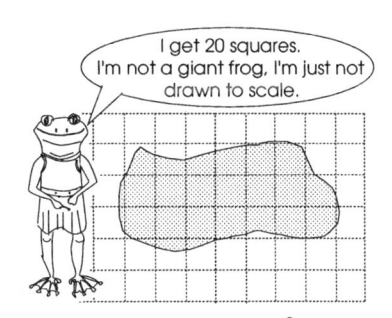

20 squares fit this description and as each square represents 4 m², the surface area must be approximately 80 m².

Area of a triangle

Area of triangle = $\frac{1}{2} \times$ base $\times$ height

(you will find this formula (and many others) at the front of the exam paper)

The triangle's measurements are only accurate enough to give the area to 1 d.p.

Calculate the area of this triangle:

$$0.5 \times 2.5 \times 3.1 = 3.875 \text{ cm}^2$$

Answer = 3.9 cm² 1 d.p.

5.7 cm
2.5 cm
h = 3.1 cm
You need the ⊥ height.

Area of a parallelogram

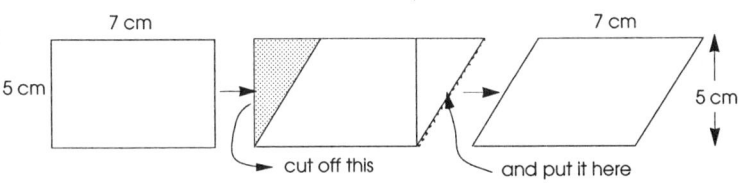

7 cm
5 cm

← cut off this   and put it here →

Area of paralellogram = base × perpendicular height
= 5 cm × 7 cm
= 35 cm²

When we are working with parallelograms and triangles we can use any side as the base but the height must be perpendicular to the base.

If you change a rectangle into a parallelogram, as I've done above, the area remains the same.

Shape and Space

Area of a trapezium

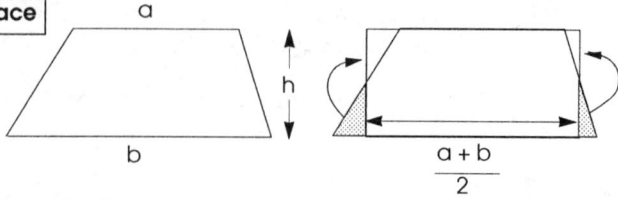

If you change this trapezium into a rectangle, its length will be the mean of the parallel sides.

$$\text{Area} = \text{length} \times \text{height}$$
$$= \frac{a+b}{2} \times h$$

or, as your exam paper will say:

$$\text{area} = \frac{1}{2}(a+b)h$$

Volume

How many cm cubes does it take to build this cuboid, i.e. what is the volume of this solid?

The bottom layer takes $6 \times 3 = 18$
There are 2 layers so the total is:
$$6 \times 3 \times 2 = 36 \text{ cm}^3$$

Volume of a cube and a cuboid

length x width x height = volume

I've used the method that is given on the exam paper.

Volume of cylinder and prisms

You can slice a cylinder or prism along a straight edge so that each slice shows a uniform cross section.

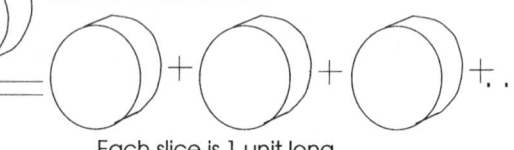

Each slice is 1 unit long.

Volume = Area of cross section x length

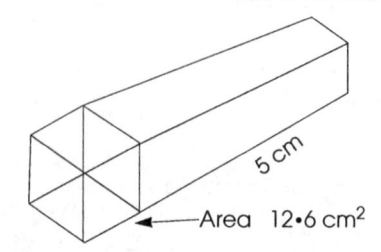

$V = 12 \cdot 6 \times 5$
$= 63 \text{ cm}^3$ = Volume of this hexagonal prism

Area 12•6 cm²

Finding the area and height or length

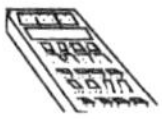

This pencil has a volume of 8·64 cm³ and a uniform cross section of 48mm². How long is it?

We need to change this to cm²

| 48 | ÷ | (| 10 | x | 10 |) |
| = | 0·48 cm² |

Volume = Area x Length

so Length = $\dfrac{\text{Volume}}{\text{Area}}$

$= \dfrac{8 \cdot 64 \text{ cm}^3}{0 \cdot 48 \text{ cm}^2}$

$= 18$ cm

This square-based cuboid has a height of 7 mm and a volume of 63 mm³.

What is the size of the base?

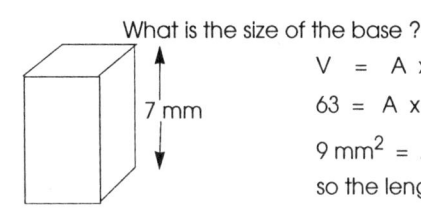

7 mm

V = A x 7
63 = A x 7
9 mm² = A   but 9 = 3 x 3
so the length of a side is 3 mm.

Liquid measure

Volumes of liquids are usually measured in litres.

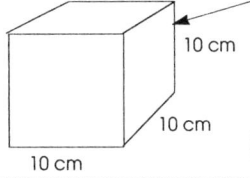

This volume is the same as 1 litre.

10 cm
10 cm
10 cm

1 litre = 10 x 10 x 10 = 1000cm³
or 1 ml = 1 cm³

(10ml = 1 cl)
(100cl = 1 litre)

1 cm³ is often written as 1 cc
1 cm³ = 1cc = 1ml

Enlargement and reduction

There are several methods by which you can enlarge or reduce shapes.

We can print similar shapes by printing different sized photos from the same negatives. Pretty obvious really. All the shapes are the same, only the sizes are different.

Using a grid

Draw a square grid over the picture.

Draw a larger grid and then copy onto it each point where the picture lines cross the grid lines and copy the shape of the curves.

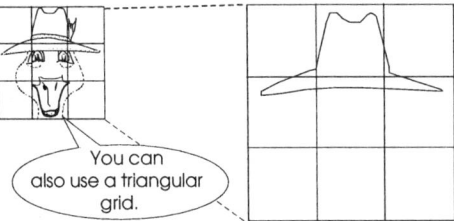

You can also use a triangular grid.

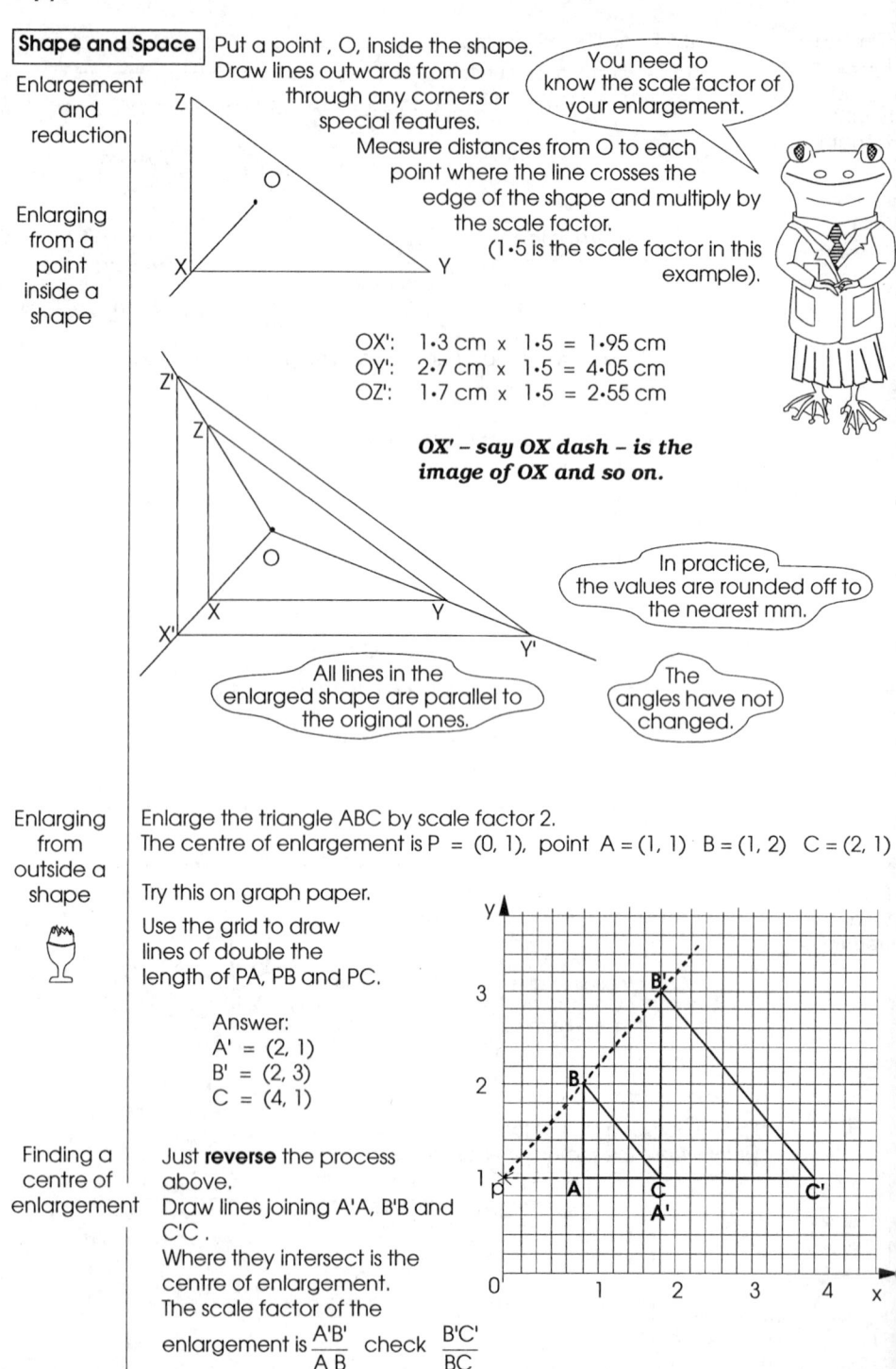

Shape and Space

Enlargement and reduction

Enlarging from a point inside a shape

Put a point, O, inside the shape. Draw lines outwards from O through any corners or special features.

Measure distances from O to each point where the line crosses the edge of the shape and multiply by the scale factor.
(1·5 is the scale factor in this example).

You need to know the scale factor of your enlargement.

OX': 1·3 cm x 1·5 = 1·95 cm
OY': 2·7 cm x 1·5 = 4·05 cm
OZ': 1·7 cm x 1·5 = 2·55 cm

OX' – say OX dash – is the image of OX and so on.

In practice, the values are rounded off to the nearest mm.

All lines in the enlarged shape are parallel to the original ones.

The angles have not changed.

Enlarging from outside a shape

Enlarge the triangle ABC by scale factor 2.
The centre of enlargement is P = (0, 1), point A = (1, 1) B = (1, 2) C = (2, 1)

Try this on graph paper.

Use the grid to draw lines of double the length of PA, PB and PC.

Answer:
A' = (2, 1)
B' = (2, 3)
C = (4, 1)

Finding a centre of enlargement

Just **reverse** the process above.

Draw lines joining A'A, B'B and C'C.

Where they intersect is the centre of enlargement.

The scale factor of the enlargement is $\dfrac{A'B'}{AB}$ check $\dfrac{B'C'}{BC}$

Fractional Enlargement

If you enlarge by a scale factor < 1 then a shape smaller than the original object will result.

These rhombi are similar (I used Pythagoras to work out the diagonals). The scale factor of $1/4$ means all the lengths in A are multiplied by $1/4$ to get the lengths of the corresponding sides in shape B.

A: 4·2 cm, 4·2 cm, 7·4

× $1/4$

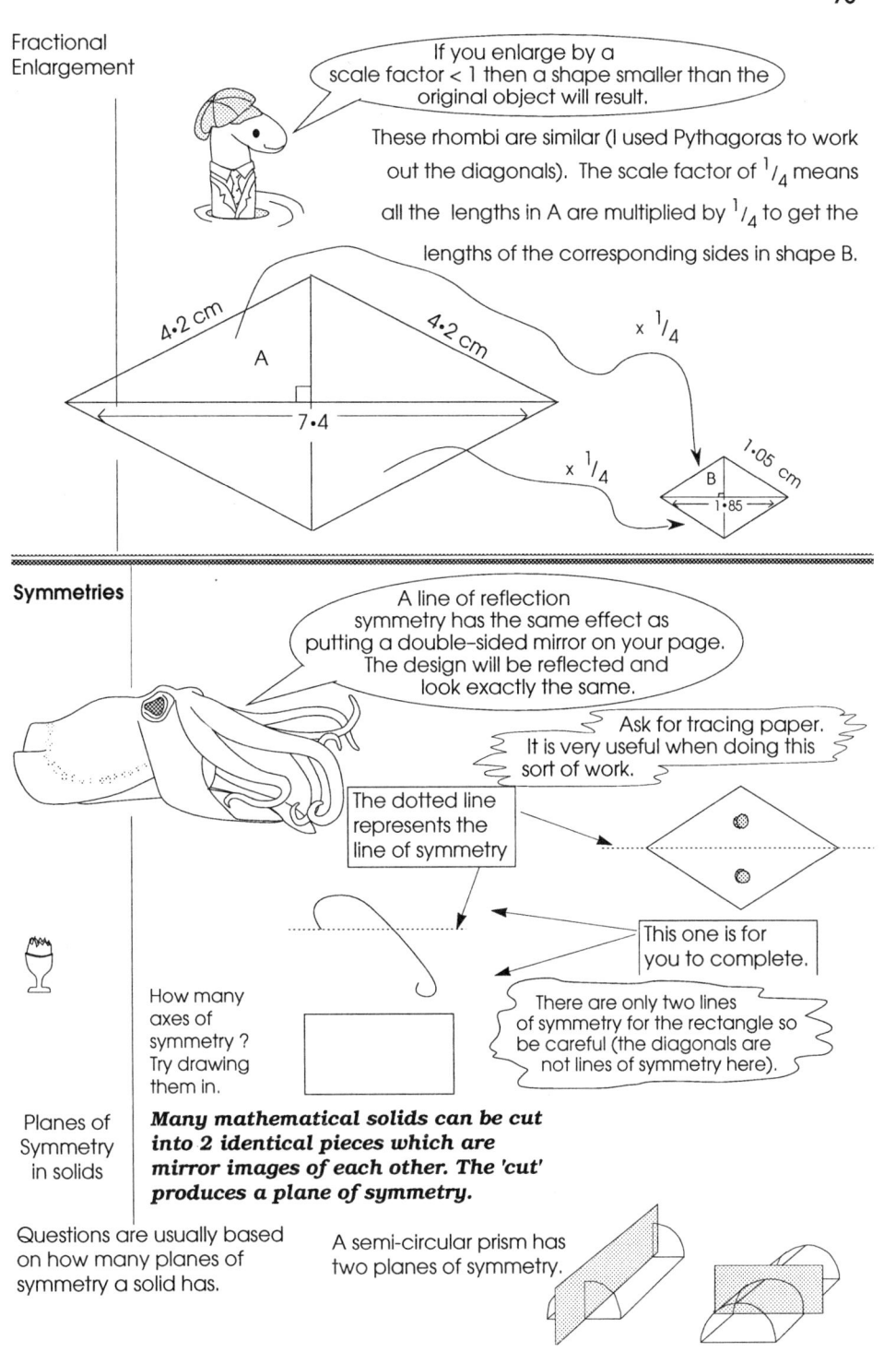

× $1/4$

B: 1·05 cm, 1·85

Symmetries

A line of reflection symmetry has the same effect as putting a double-sided mirror on your page. The design will be reflected and look exactly the same.

Ask for tracing paper. It is very useful when doing this sort of work.

The dotted line represents the line of symmetry

This one is for you to complete.

How many axes of symmetry? Try drawing them in.

There are only two lines of symmetry for the rectangle so be careful (the diagonals are not lines of symmetry here).

Planes of Symmetry in solids

Many mathematical solids can be cut into 2 identical pieces which are mirror images of each other. The 'cut' produces a plane of symmetry.

Questions are usually based on how many planes of symmetry a solid has.

A semi-circular prism has two planes of symmetry.

Shape and Space

Planes of symmetry (continued)

In any prism there is one plane parallel to the cross section and then those which match the lines of symmetry on the cross section.

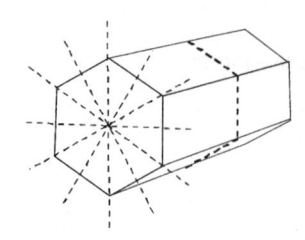

A hexagonal prism has
$1 + 6 = 7$ planes of symmetry

Planes of symmetry in any solid

Imagine making the solid of marzipan or dough.
Cut it with a knife into pieces which are reflections of each other.
The number of correct cuts is the number of planes of symmetry.

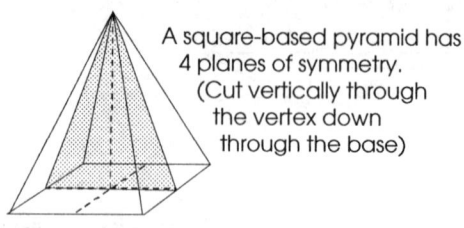

A square-based pyramid has 4 planes of symmetry.
(Cut vertically through the vertex down through the base)

Finding a mirror line

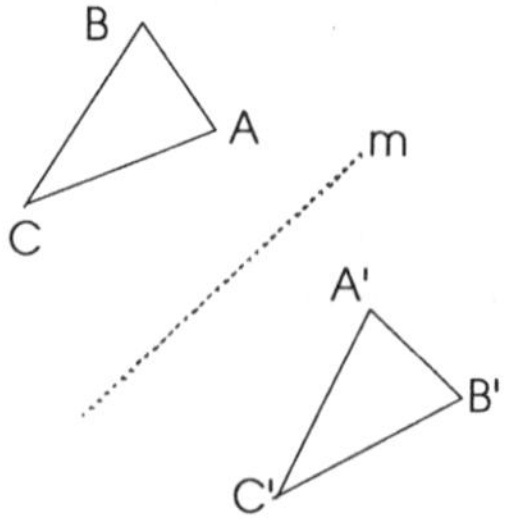

Object ABC is mapped onto image A' B' C' by a reflection in line m.

The mirror line is a perpendicular bisector of AA', BB' and CC'.

Use compasses to draw these

Reflection in a grid

Using graph paper for reflections implies that lines defined by equations will be used as lines of symmetry such as: $y = x$, $x + y = 0$, $x = a$, $y = b$.

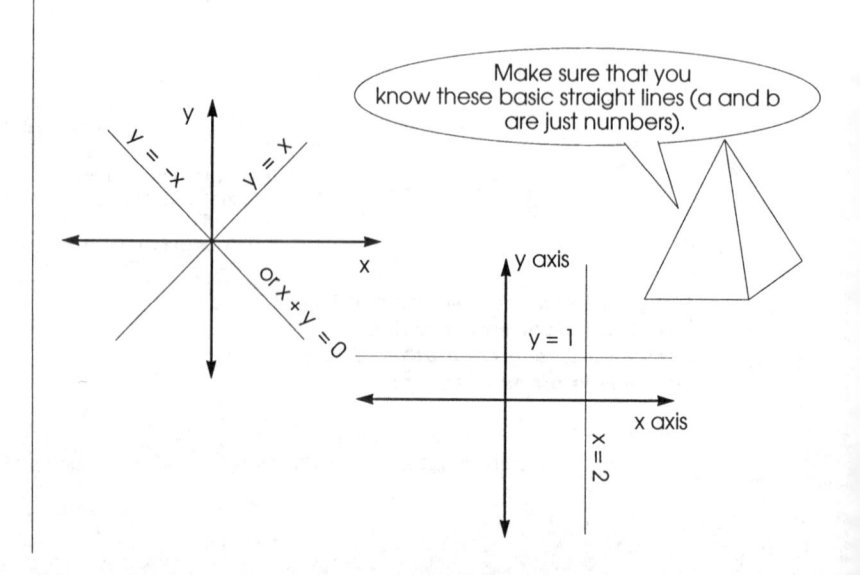

Make sure that you know these basic straight lines (a and b are just numbers).

$y = -x$ $y = x$

or $x + y = 0$

$y = 1$

$x = 2$

Reflection in a grid (continued)

The quadrilateral ABCD is reflected in the line $y = 2$.
The image is A'B'C'D'.
What are the coordinates of C' ?

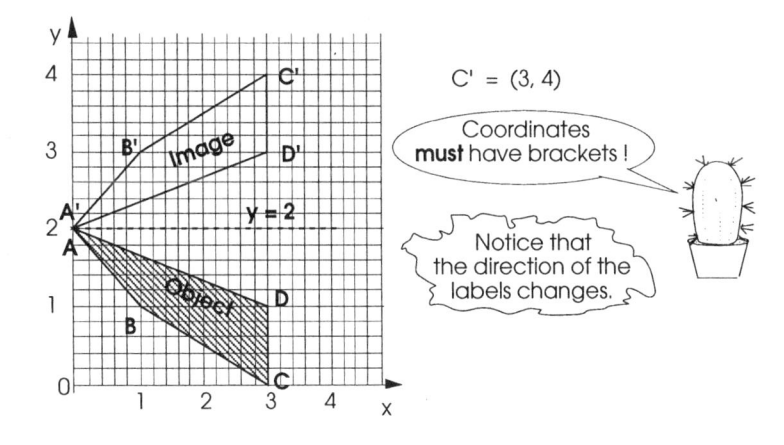

C' = (3, 4)

Coordinates **must** have brackets !

Notice that the direction of the labels changes.

Rotational symmetry

If a shape is rotated about a point (the centre of rotation) and it fits exactly onto itself as you turn it round, you have rotational symmetry.

This shape fits onto itself twice so we say it has symmetry order 2. (a)

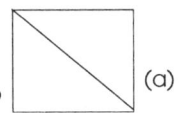

This shape has rotation order 3. (b)

Centre of rotation

When a plane is rotated the only point which does not move is called the centre of rotation.

This is the point where you hold down the tracing paper with a pencil and turn the paper.

Angle of rotation

We can calculate the angle through which the two objects above were rotated.

a. $360° \div 2 = 180°$ b. $360° \div 3 = 120°$

The shapes in (a) and (b) fitted onto themselves but in the next example the shapes are rotated and produce an image.

Note that the centre of rotation is not in the centre of the object

Shape and Space

Rotations on a grid

Rotate triangle A through 90° anti-clockwise about the origin.

Method

1. Join a vertex to the point (0, 0) and trace the diagram A including the axes.
2. Put pencil point on the origin and turn the tracing paper around 90° anticlockwise i.e. until x axis maps onto y axis.

Get some tracing paper and try it now. Just reading through is not the same as remembering.

Every line in the image is at 90° to the corresponding line in the object.

To remember things you need to have a go. Take it from a sheep who knows.

Finding the centre and angle of a rotation

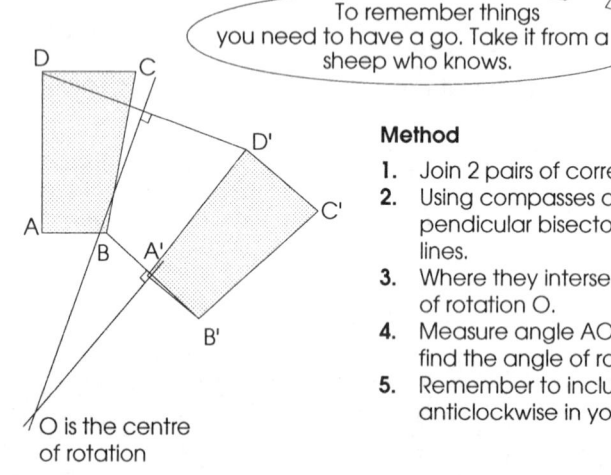

O is the centre of rotation

Method

1. Join 2 pairs of corresponding points.
2. Using compasses construct the perpendicular bisectors of the joining lines.
3. Where they intersect is the centre of rotation O.
4. Measure angle AOA' or BOB' etc. to find the angle of ration.
5. Remember to include clockwise or anticlockwise in your answer.

Summary of transformations

The four transformations must be explained or defined in full detail if you are to gain full marks.

The table below tells you exactly how much detail you need to write down as well as the **name** of the transformation.

Reflection	Rotation	Enlargement	Translation
draw mirrorline give equation if possible.	name centre of rotation, angle and direction	state centre of enlargement and scale factor	$\begin{bmatrix} x \\ y \end{bmatrix}$ give the vector in numbers

(Continued)

Combinations of translations

Combining any transformations gives 16 possible pairs and there is no need to give such a long list.

Make sure you draw clear diagram and follow through the movements in order.

Write down the **single** transformation which maps the objects onto the final image.

Useful results

a. Two reflections 'cancel' each other out. The result of two reflections is a rotation or a translation.
b. Two translations results in one translation '- just add the vectors.
c. Two enlargements using the same centre of enlargement gives an enlargement with the scale factors **multiplied** together.

Vectors

A vector is something that has both size (magnitude) and direction.

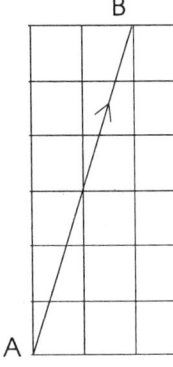

A vector does not tell you where you should start, it just tells you where to go once you have started.

e.g. $\begin{bmatrix} 2 \\ 6 \end{bmatrix}$ is a column vector (the information is given in a column).

The top number says 'move two units to the right',

The bottom number says 'move six units up'.

The $\begin{bmatrix} m \\ n \end{bmatrix}$ convention for movement is just like that used for co-ordinates:

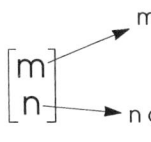

m carries instructions for a move to right or left
negative to the left, positive to the right   −ve ← +ve →

$\begin{bmatrix} m \\ n \end{bmatrix}$

n carries instructions for a move up or down
negative moves down,
positive moves up   ↑ +ve   ↓ −ve

The arrow over AB just shows that the vector starts at A and finishes at B.

$\overrightarrow{AB} = \begin{pmatrix} 2 \\ 6 \end{pmatrix}$

Round brackets are also used.

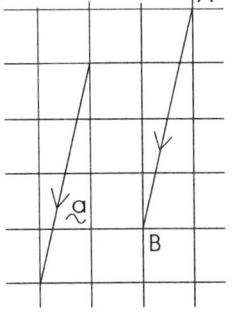

Another way of describing the vector AB is to use $\underset{\sim}{a}$ (a lower case letter with a squiggle beneath it).

i.e. $\overrightarrow{AB} = \underset{\sim}{a} = \begin{bmatrix} -1 \\ -4 \end{bmatrix}$

also $\underline{a}$ or **a** (in bold).

Shape and Space

Inverse of a vector

The inverse of a vector is a vector of the same magnitude but in the opposite direction.

$$\underset{\sim}{d} = \begin{bmatrix} 1 \\ 2 \end{bmatrix} \quad \underset{\sim}{-d} = \begin{bmatrix} -1 \\ -2 \end{bmatrix}$$

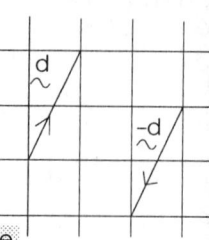

Translations that are defined by vectors

In a translation every point in the plane moves the same distance and in the same direction. The information may be given as a vector quantity.

This diagram shows the image of the triangle ABC translated through $\begin{bmatrix} 2 \\ -1 \end{bmatrix}$

$$\overrightarrow{AA'} = \overrightarrow{BB'} = \overrightarrow{CC'} = \begin{bmatrix} 2 \\ -1 \end{bmatrix}$$

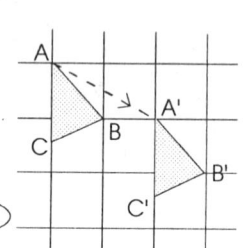

The first thing we need to do is decide when shapes or solids are considered to be similar:

Shapes and solids are similar when:
corresponding angles are equal and
the ratio of corresponding sides is the same.

This ratio is called the scale factor.

Have a look at the 2 shapes M and N. I have set out how you can work out the scale factor from the measurements

Calculating scale factors

Measure both long sides (or both short sides) i.e. you must use corresponding sides.

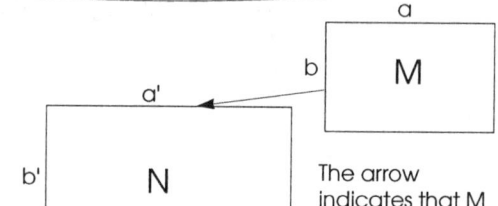

The arrow indicates that M maps onto N.

Now divide the new length from N by the old length from M :

$$\frac{a'}{a} \quad \text{or} \quad \frac{b'}{b} \quad \text{or} \quad \frac{\text{Where you go}}{\text{Where you come from}}$$

– 81 –

Calculating an unknown side

If photograph A is an enlargement of photo B, what length should the missing side be?

First find the linear scale factor

$$\frac{15}{6} = 2.5$$

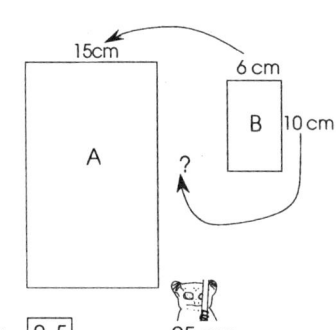

the unknown side = $\boxed{10}$ × $\boxed{2.5}$ = 25 cm

Alternative method

Ratio of $\dfrac{\text{long side}}{\text{short side}} = \dfrac{10}{6} = \dfrac{?}{15}$

$\Rightarrow \quad ? = \dfrac{10 \times 15}{6} = 25 \text{ cm}$

One-way stretches

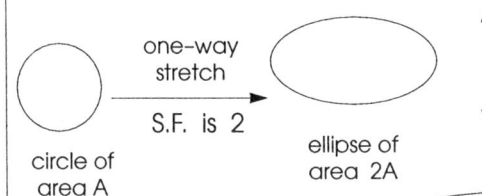

circle of area A — one-way stretch S.F. is 2 → ellipse of area 2A — one-way stretch S.F. is 2 → circle of area 4A

Remember that scale factor is applied to lengths.

Calculating lengths and angles in triangles

Sometimes we have details about triangles (like 2 angles and a side, 2 sides and an angle) and are asked to work out the other sides and angles.

This is called 'solving the triangle'.

We work these out using Pythagoras' rule or trigonometry.

Shape and Space

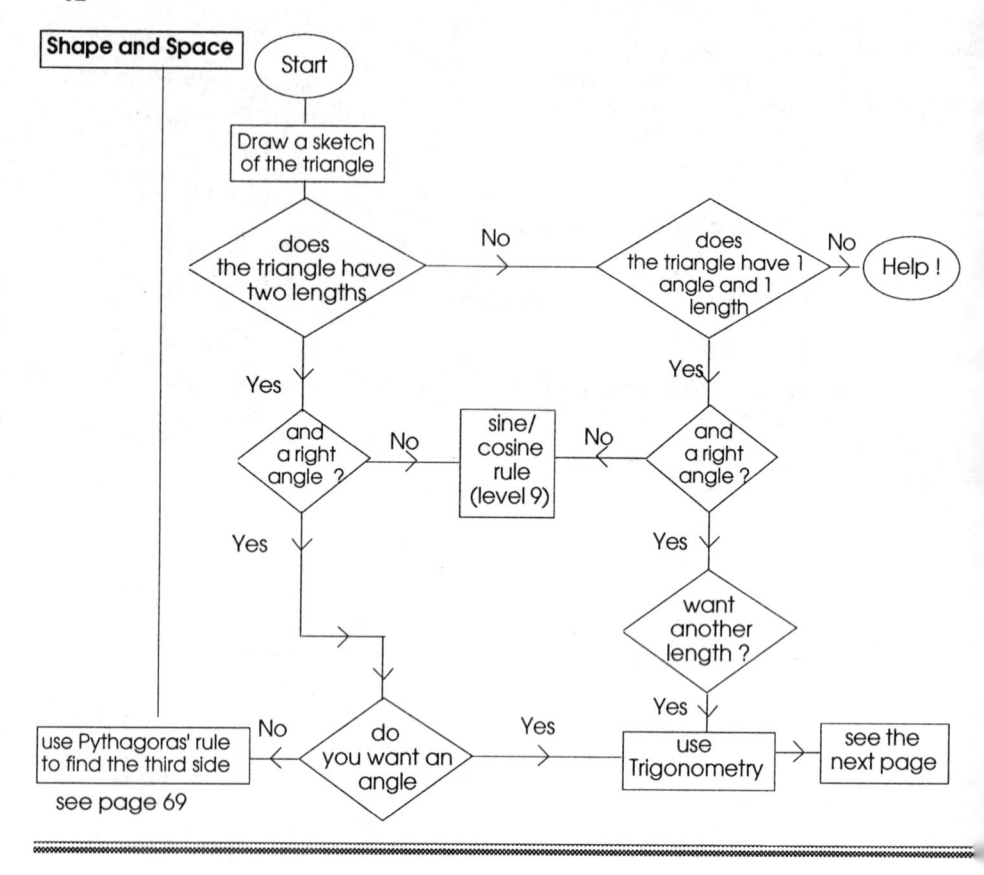

```
Start
  │
  ▼
Draw a sketch
of the triangle
  │
  ▼
does the triangle have two lengths ──No──▶ does the triangle have 1 angle and 1 length ──No──▶ Help !
  │                                              │
  Yes                                            Yes
  ▼                                              ▼
and a right angle ? ──No──▶ sine/cosine rule (level 9) ◀──No── and a right angle ?
  │                                                              │
  Yes                                                            Yes
  ▼                                                              ▼
  │                                                         want another length ?
  │                                                              │
  ▼                                                             Yes
do you want an angle ──Yes──▶ use Trigonometry ──▶ see the next page
  │
  No
  ▼
use Pythagoras' rule to find the third side
see page 69
```

Trigonometry

Every right angled triangle is an enlargement of another triangle with hypotenuse of length 1 unit.

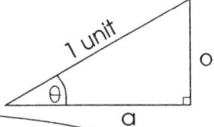

Once we have the formulae shown below we can use a calculator to work out the values of o and a.

SOH CAH TOA

$\sin \theta = \dfrac{\text{Opposite}}{\text{Hypotenuse}}$

$\cos \theta = \dfrac{\text{Adjacent}}{\text{Hypotenuse}}$

$\tan \theta = \dfrac{\text{Opposite}}{\text{Adjacent}}$

or

opp = hyp × sin θ
adj = hyp × cos θ
opp = adj × tan θ

Most of us are happy to forget that we are using enlargements and just remember how to substitute values into the equations.

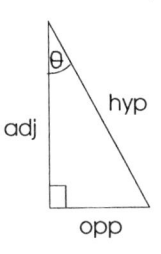

The adjacent side touches the angle, the hypotenuse is always opposite the right angle.

Label the sides after you have identified the angle you know or want (θ).

Next, decide which of the above equations uses two of the values given in the question.

When calculating sides, use the trig. button.

Write the equation down and then substitute in the values given, rearrange if necessary and then do the calculations.

For the angles, use the inverse trig. buttons.

To find a side

To find x :

Label sides : opp and hypotenuse ⟹ 5 cm

$\sin \theta = \dfrac{\text{opp}}{\text{hyp}}$

$\sin 79° = \dfrac{\text{opp}}{3 \cdot 2}$

You find this on the formula sheet at the front of the exam paper.

$3 \cdot 2 \times \boxed{\sin} \boxed{79} = \boxed{x}$

On some calculators you may need to enter: $\boxed{79} \boxed{\text{Sin}}$

x = 3·14 cm
correct to 3 sig. fig.

Shape and Space

1

Triangle with Opp. = 7.4 mm, Hyp. = y, angle 36°

To find y ... opp and hyp ⟹ Sin

$$\sin 36° = \frac{7.44}{y}$$ multiply by y

$$y \times \sin 36° = 7.44$$ divide by sin 36

$$y = \frac{7.44}{\sin 36}$$

$$y = 12.7 \text{ mm}$$

Always write your answers on the diagram as well and then you will notice if you have made a silly mistake like calculating a hypotenuse shorter than an opposite or adjacent side.

Isosceles triangles

Remember to draw in the line of symmetry so that you have a right angle triangle to work with before you use SOHCAMTOA. (There is a question on this at the back.)

Angles of elevation and depression often crop up in trigonometry questions.

Angles of elevation and depression

- a person on the cliff
- angle of elevation
- horizontal line
- angle of depression
- horizontal line
- x

x is alternate angle to the angle of depression so it is equal to angle of depression.

2

A tower block is viewed from 1·6 km away. The angle of elevation of the top of the tower block is 4°.
How high is the building?

A diagram is essential here.

— 4° 1·6 km h

Let h = height of the tower block.

$$\tan \theta = \frac{\text{opp}}{\text{adj}}$$

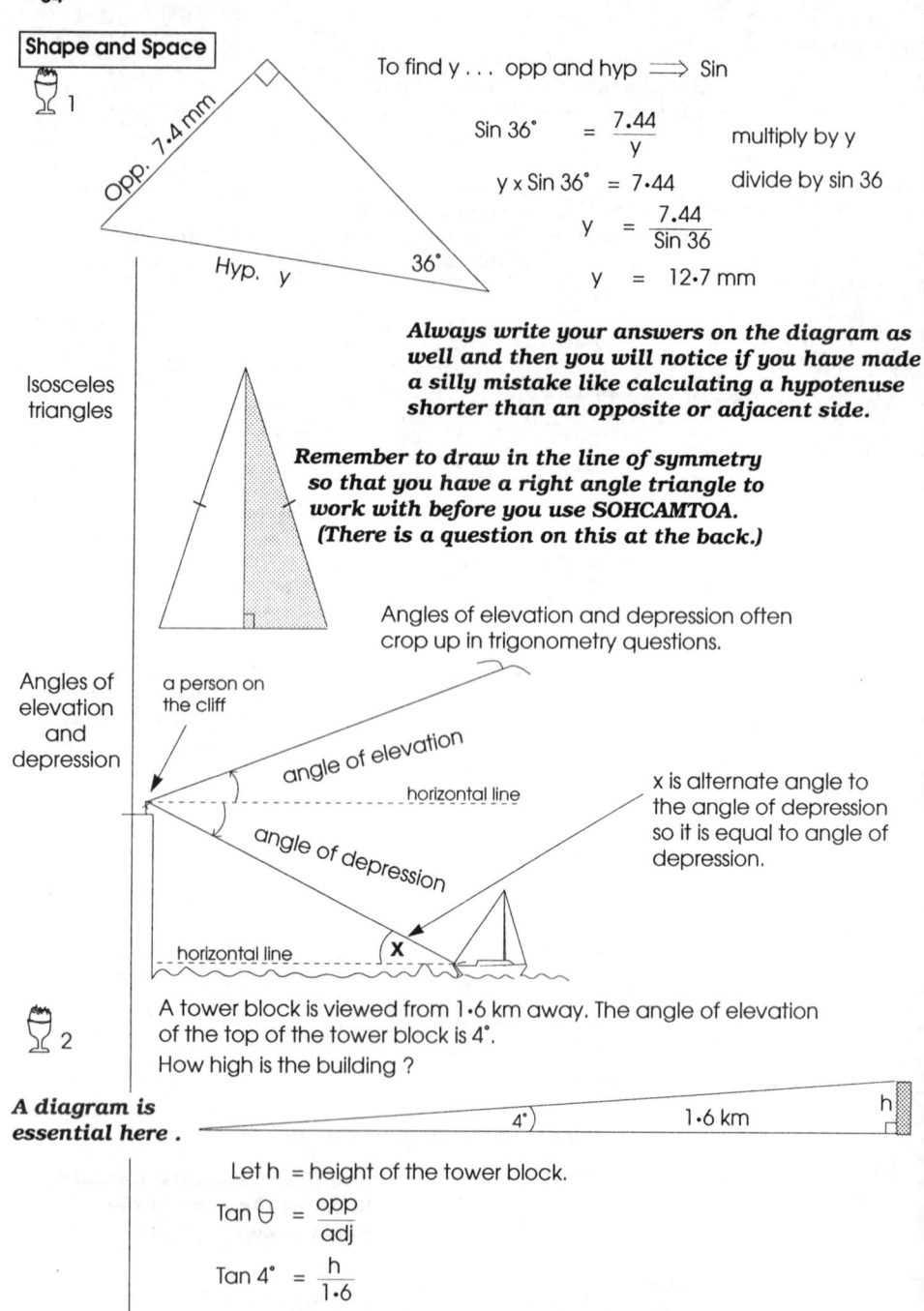

$$\tan 4° = \frac{h}{1·6}$$

$$1·6 \times \tan 4° = h$$
$$h = 0·0699 \text{ km}$$
$$h = 69·9 \text{ m}$$

- 85 -

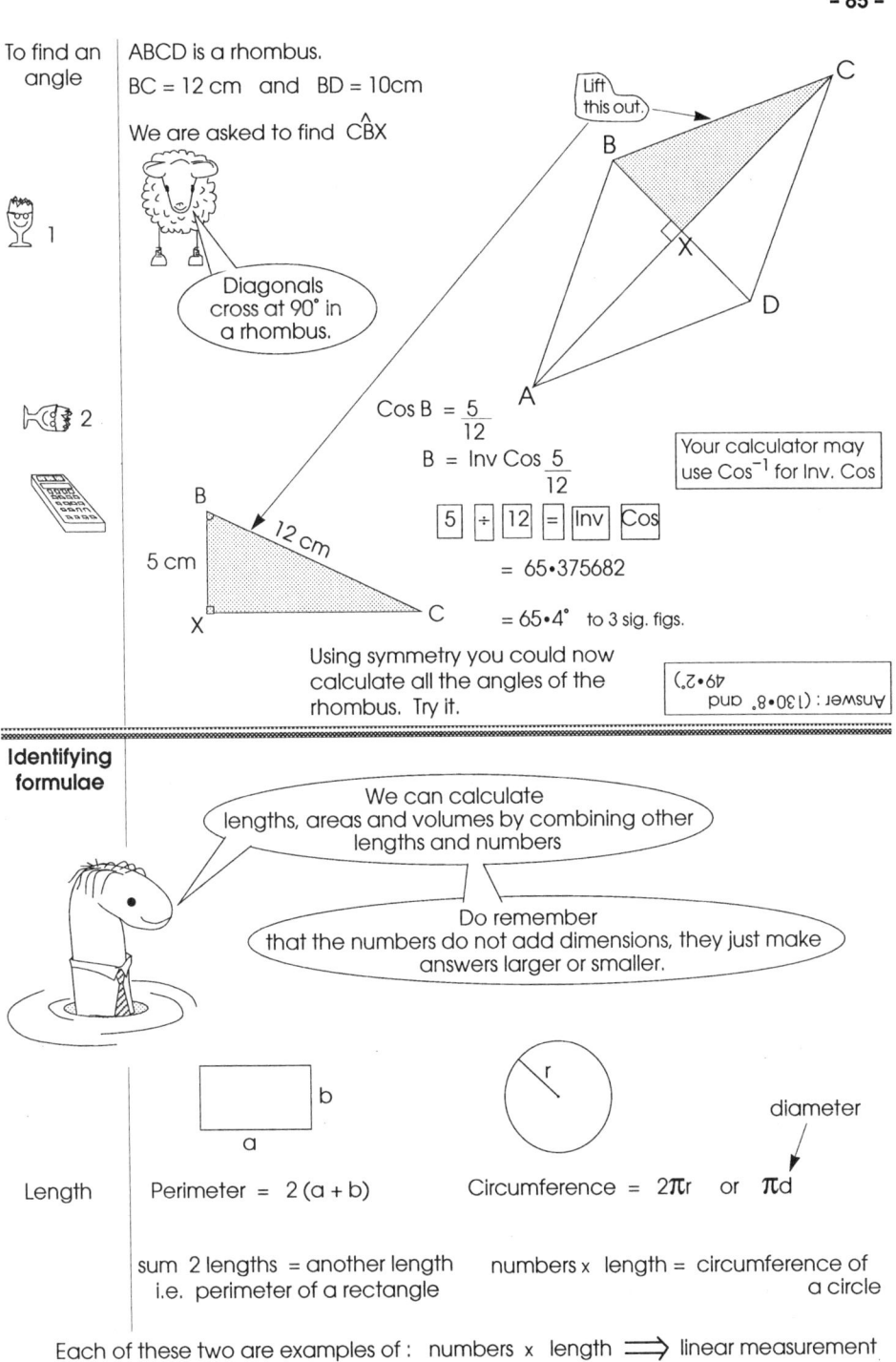

To find an angle	ABCD is a rhombus. BC = 12 cm and BD = 10cm We are asked to find CB̂X

1 — Diagonals cross at 90° in a rhombus.

2

$$\cos B = \frac{5}{12}$$

$$B = \text{Inv Cos } \frac{5}{12}$$

Your calculator may use $\cos^{-1}$ for Inv. Cos

5 ÷ 12 = Inv Cos

= 65·375682

= 65·4° to 3 sig. figs.

Using symmetry you could now calculate all the angles of the rhombus. Try it.

Answer: (130·8° and 49·2°)

Identifying formulae

We can calculate lengths, areas and volumes by combining other lengths and numbers

Do remember that the numbers do not add dimensions, they just make answers larger or smaller.

Length | Perimeter = 2(a + b) | Circumference = $2\pi r$ or πd

sum 2 lengths = another length
i.e. perimeter of a rectangle

numbers × length = circumference of a circle

Each of these two are examples of : numbers × length ⟹ linear measurement

Shape and Space

Area

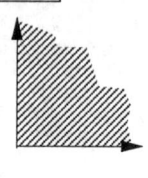

Area is defined by 2 dimensions <u>usually</u> at right angles to each other.

Area of $\triangle$ = $\frac{1}{2}$ base × height   Area of $\bigcirc$ = πr^2

↑ number   ↑ length × length   ↑ number   ↑ length × length

$4\pi r^2$ r^2 i.e. r × r i.e. 2 lengths – it's the <u>surface area of a sphere</u>
               (4 and π are numbers)

$\frac{4}{3}\pi r^3$ r^3 i.e. r × r × r i.e. 3 lengths – Its the volume of a sphere

r × r × r spans 3 dimensions so we are dealing with volume

> Have another look at page 72 for details on calculating the volume of cylinders and prisms

Sometimes a length is written in the denominator and has the effect of cancelling out a length in the numerator.
e.g.

$$\frac{\pi r^2 h}{l} = \frac{\text{number} \times \text{dimension} \times \text{dimension} \times \text{dimension}}{\text{dimension}}$$

This gives only two dimensions and so could only represent an **area**.

If a, b and c are lengths, which of the following formulae represent volumes?

i. $2a^3$ ii. $\pi a(a+b)$ iii. $\frac{abc^2}{a}$ iv. $4\pi b^2 c$

Answers: i. iii. and iv.

Space for you notes.

Handling Data | AT 4

Don't be put off by all those jokes about lies, damned lies and statistics. Statistics can be misused but they are also hugely useful in helping us make decisions when the answer is not clear cut.

e.g. displaying as a table, diagram or graph or summarising it using special statistical words..

Statistics involves collecting data and describing it in a way that makes it easy to understand.

The trends are then more easily picked out.

Statistics Statistics are there to allow us to see past the confusion of many figures. They help us spot the patterns.

Data Data is collected for different reasons:

Market research — A company may find out public taste before introducing a new biscuit.

Quality control — Once the biscuit is in production the biscuits are checked for quality.

Information, records and reference — Record regional sales of the biscuit to assist with dispatch, advertising campaigns etc.

Types of data Data can be of various types:

Qualitative data — Qualitative data tends to be given as words. e.g. people's favourite colour or the make of car that people own.

Quantitative data — Quantitative data tends to be given as numbers. e.g. heights of sunflower plants, number of pupils in a class.

Quantitative data can be either discrete or continuous.

Discrete data — In the case of discrete data all the possible values can be listed. e.g. the number of goals scored in a game could be 0, 1, 2, 3, . . . or shoe sizes could be . . . 3, $3\frac{1}{2}$, 4, $4\frac{1}{2}$, . . .

Continuous data — Continuous data can take any value in a certain range. e.g. a sunflower plant is 30cm tall one day and 45cm tall a week later. The plant must have measured all the values between 30cm and 45cm during the week.

Continuous data often deals with measurements.

Continuous data can only be as accurate as the measuring device used to do the measuring.

Continuous

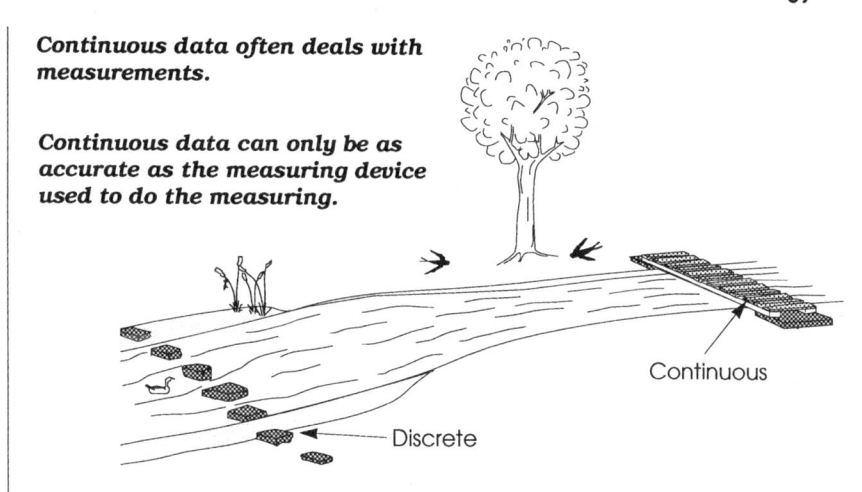

Discrete

Collecting data

We can collect data in a number of ways:-

refer to data already recorded	This information could be in tables e.g. two-way tables, computer data bases etc.
by observation	e.g. we might investigate the behaviour of babies by watching them and taking notes.
by using sampling methods	e.g. it might not be possible to collect data from every source so sensible samples are taken.
by using questionnaires	Great care is needed when designing the questionnaire: - decide exactly what you want to find out - then use direct, easy-to-answer questions.

More on questionnaires

Do not ask embarrassing questions (if only because you are less likely to get truthful answers),

e.g. ' Have you read a book in the last month?' is too vague.
' How many books have you read in the last month ?
Choose from: 0, 1, 2, more than 2.' is much better.

e.g. ' You don't smoke do you?' suggests that you should not smoke.
The question is biased.
' Do you smoke ?' Yes ☐   No ☐   is much better.

It is a good idea to test the questionnaire out on a small sample to check that the questions are understood in the way you meant them to be.

You will be amazed at how questions which seem so simple can be understood in several different ways.

| Handling Data | AT 4 |

| Hypothesis | It is often easiest to begin with a hypothesis (your theory for something e.g. left-handed people are cleverer than right-handed people) and then test it.
The hypothesis can be tested by designing an appropriate questionnaire or by devising a suitable method for testing it. The data can be collected from everybody of from a sample that represents everybody.

How the collected data is processed is critical– the results must be interpreted in a fair and unbiased way! |

| Presenting data | Presenting data in the form of a diagram often makes it much easier to interpret. |

| Pictograms | Discrete data is usually presented as pictograms or bar charts. Pictures or symbols are used to represent the data. |

A pictogram showing the attendance at school during one week (Class 43b)

Monday	🧒🧒🧒🧒🧒
Tuesday	🧒🧒🧒🧒🧒🧒
Wednesday	🧒🧒🧒🧒
Thursday	🧒🧒🧒🧒🧒
Friday	🧒🧒🧒🧒🧒

Remember to give a key. Explain what each symbol represents

🧒 4 pupils
🧒 3 pupils
🧒 2 pupils
🧒 1 pupil

| Data display
Bar graph or bar chart | A bar graph is a set of rectangles whose heights represent quantities. The idea is to present results in a way that makes them easier to understand and easier to take in at a glance. |

I've drawn a bar chart of shoe size (everyone had to state the nearest whole size). The chart deals with all the pupils who are 11 years old.

We separate the bars to show that shoe size is not continuous.

| Distributions | If snake had drawn a bar chart of shoe sizes of the 15–16 year olds we would expect the same shape of chart but the mode would be higher for a larger shoes size.

This shape (like a bell) occurs in many analyses. Sparrow wing sizes, pig body weights, leaf sizes, body temperatures etc. give the bell shape when the frequencies are plotted. |

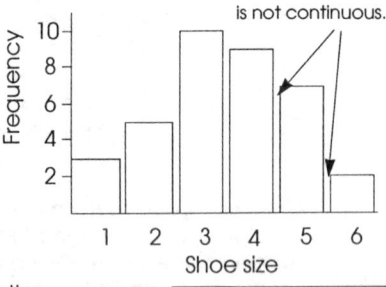

Frequency vs Shoe size (1–6)

Bar charts may be drawn vertically or horizontally.

Bar-line graphs

Hours of sunshine in Norwich during 1 week in August

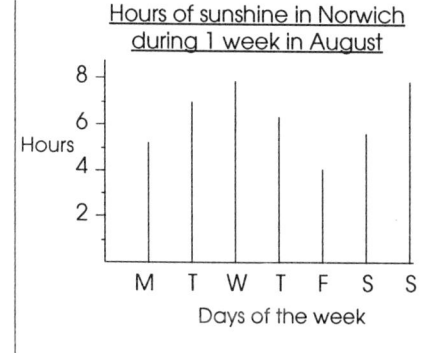

Hours (vertical axis: 2, 4, 6, 8) vs Days of the week (M T W T F S S)

Vertical lines are drawn instead of bars. Remember to label the horizontal axis **under** each vertical line.

Pie charts

Pie chart showing the ingredients in a particular stew

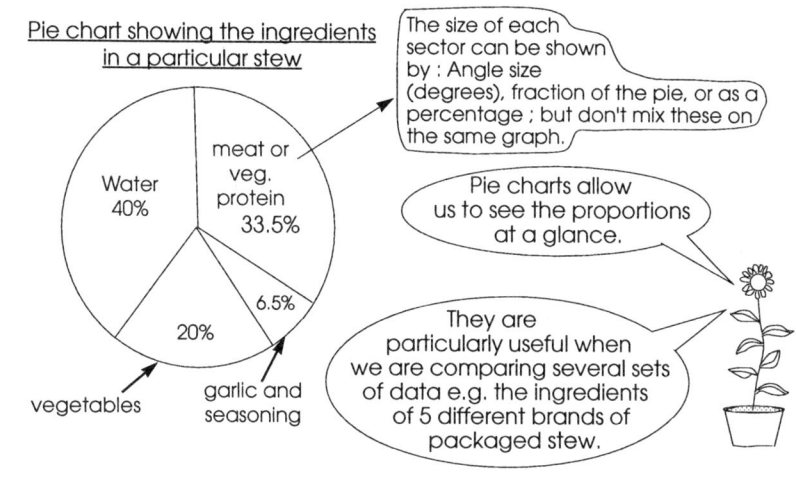

- Water 40%
- meat or veg. protein 33.5%
- vegetables 20%
- garlic and seasoning 6.5%

The size of each sector can be shown by: Angle size (degrees), fraction of the pie, or as a percentage; but don't mix these on the same graph.

Pie charts allow us to see the proportions at a glance.

They are particularly useful when we are comparing several sets of data e.g. the ingredients of 5 different brands of packaged stew.

Line graphs

Continuous data is usually presented as line graphs, frequency diagrams or histograms.

The height of a sunflower plant was measured every day for a week.

Day	Mon.	Tues.	Wed.	Thurs.	Fri.	Sat.	Sun.
Height in cm	35	37	38	40	41	43	46

Graph showing how the height of a sunflower plant changed over a week

(Left graph: Height in cm, scale 0–50, plotted against M T W T F S S)

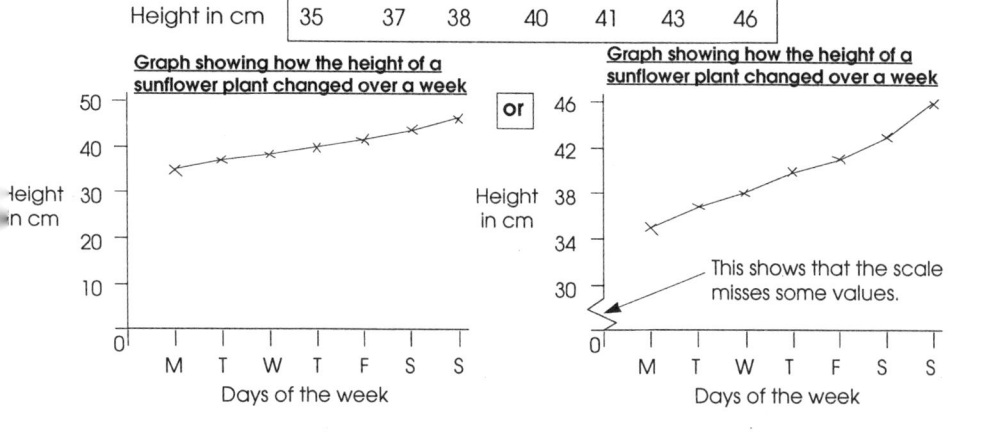

or

Graph showing how the height of a sunflower plant changed over a week

(Right graph: Height in cm, scale 30–46, plotted against M T W T F S S)

This shows that the scale misses some values.

Handling Data | AT 4

Frequency diagrams

Continuous data needs bar charts without spaces between the bars. They are often incorrectly called histograms.

I've got Snake to draw up a frequency table for weights of people in school.

She decided that anybody who is exactly on the boundary of an interval is counted in the higher group

Frequency diagrams

Weight in kg	Frequency
50–55	35
55–60	46
60–65	52
65–70	55
70–75	44
75–80	29

In a histogram the <u>area</u> of each block represents the frequency. In your exams, the class intervals are of equal width – so the heights of the columns are in proportion to their frequencies.

Grouped frequency distributions

Large quantities of data is often put into convenient groups called classes.

Seedling height to the nearest cm	5 - 9	10 - 14	15 - 19	20 - 24	25 - 29
No. of plants	2	1	4	5	3

A histogram to show the range of heights reached by beech seedlings in 40 square metres of Hungarian forest measured to the nearest cm.

Note this is continuous data – Class 15 - 19 really means $14 \cdot 5 \leq$ height $< 19 \cdot 5$

Frequency polygons

Frequency polygons contain the same information as a histogram but look different because the midpoints of the top of each block have been joined up.

It might be helpful to plot 2 frequency polygons on the same axes – i.e. compare boys pocket money with girls.

This is done on the next page.

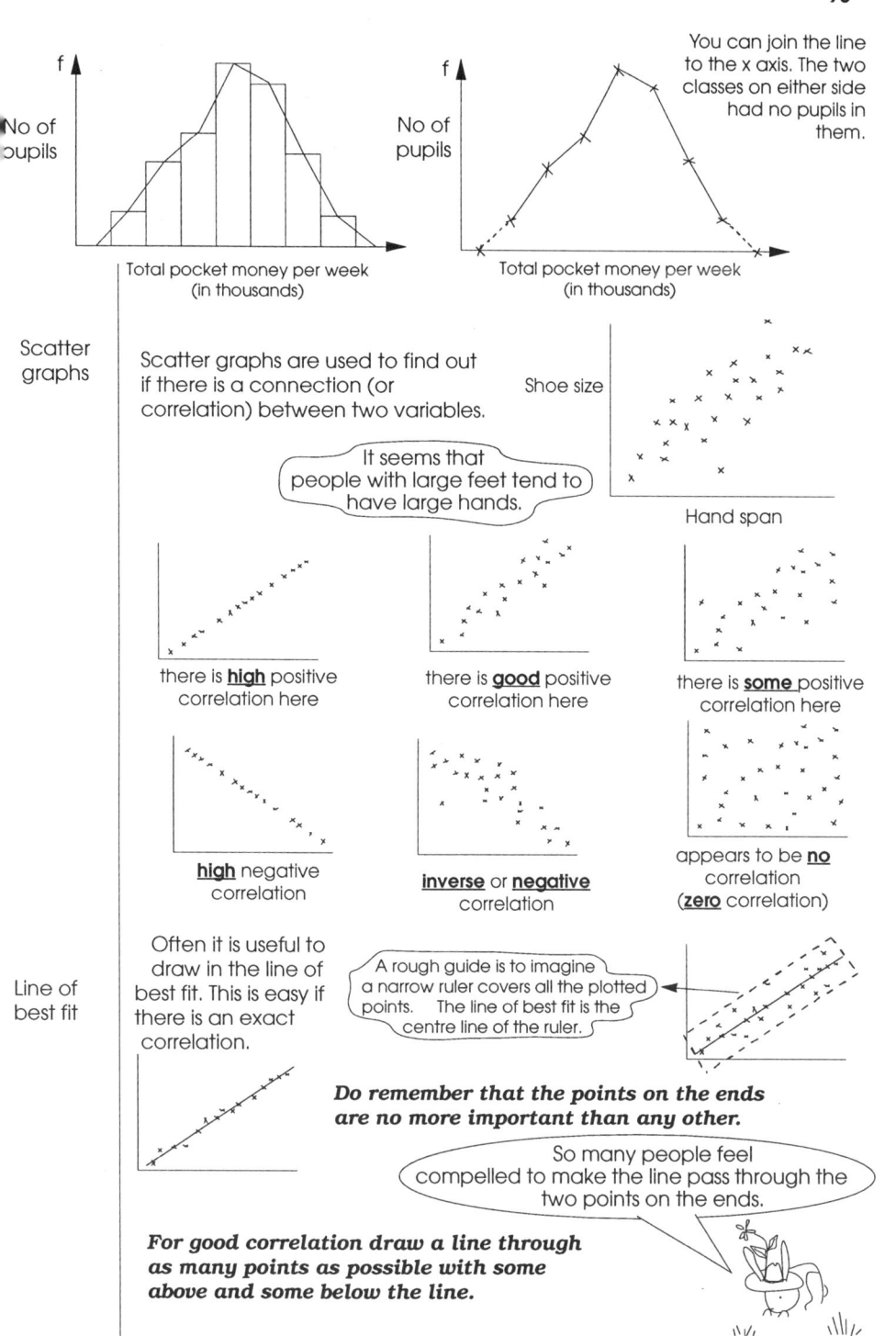

You can join the line to the x axis. The two classes on either side had no pupils in them.

(left graph) No of pupils (f) vs Total pocket money per week (in thousands)

(right graph) No of pupils (f) vs Total pocket money per week (in thousands)

Scatter graphs

Scatter graphs are used to find out if there is a connection (or correlation) between two variables.

(scatter graph: Shoe size vs Hand span)

It seems that people with large feet tend to have large hands.

there is **high** positive correlation here

there is **good** positive correlation here

there is **some** positive correlation here

high negative correlation

inverse or **negative** correlation

appears to be **no** correlation (**zero** correlation)

Line of best fit

Often it is useful to draw in the line of best fit. This is easy if there is an exact correlation.

A rough guide is to imagine a narrow ruler covers all the plotted points. The line of best fit is the centre line of the ruler.

Do remember that the points on the ends are no more important than any other.

So many people feel compelled to make the line pass through the two points on the ends.

For good correlation draw a line through as many points as possible with some above and some below the line.

Handling Data | AT 4

Cumulative frequency

> Frequency distribution tables may be rewritten to give the running total up to the end of each class interval. This is the cumulative frequency.

height in (cm)	81–100	101–120	121–140	141–160	161–180	181–200	201–220
Frequency	9	23	37	59	42	22	8

This can be rewritten as:

We'll start by looking at some totally absorbing statistics on sunflower heights.

Frequency table to show the distribution of heights of sunflower plants – (to the nearest cm).

height (cm)	cumulative frequency (f)
81–100	9
101–120	23
121–140	37
141–160	59
161–180	42
181–200	22
201–220	8
total (Σf)	200

Data can be used to prepare diagrams e.g. bar charts, scatter diagrams etc., which help us analyse the results.

Rewriting the data as a cumulative frequency table

height	frequency	upper bound	cumulative frequency
h < 80·5	0	80·5	0
80·5 ≤ h < 100·5	9	100·5	9
100·5 ≤ h < 120·5	23	120·5	32
120·5 ≤ h < 140·5	37	140·5	69
140·5 ≤ h < 160·5	59	160·5	128
160·5 ≤ h < 180·5	42	180·5	170
180·5 ≤ h < 200·5	22	200·5	192
200·5 ≤ h < 220·5	8	220·5	200

The 'less than' could be written with a < sign e.g. <160.

Write upper bound and cumulative frequency side by side then they look like 'co-ordinates' when plotting the graph.

You need to check that this value is the total.

this shows how many sunflowers altogether are less than 120·5 cm in height (i.e. 9 + 23)

> When these values are plotted as a cumulative frequency curve it is called an ogive.

Representing data

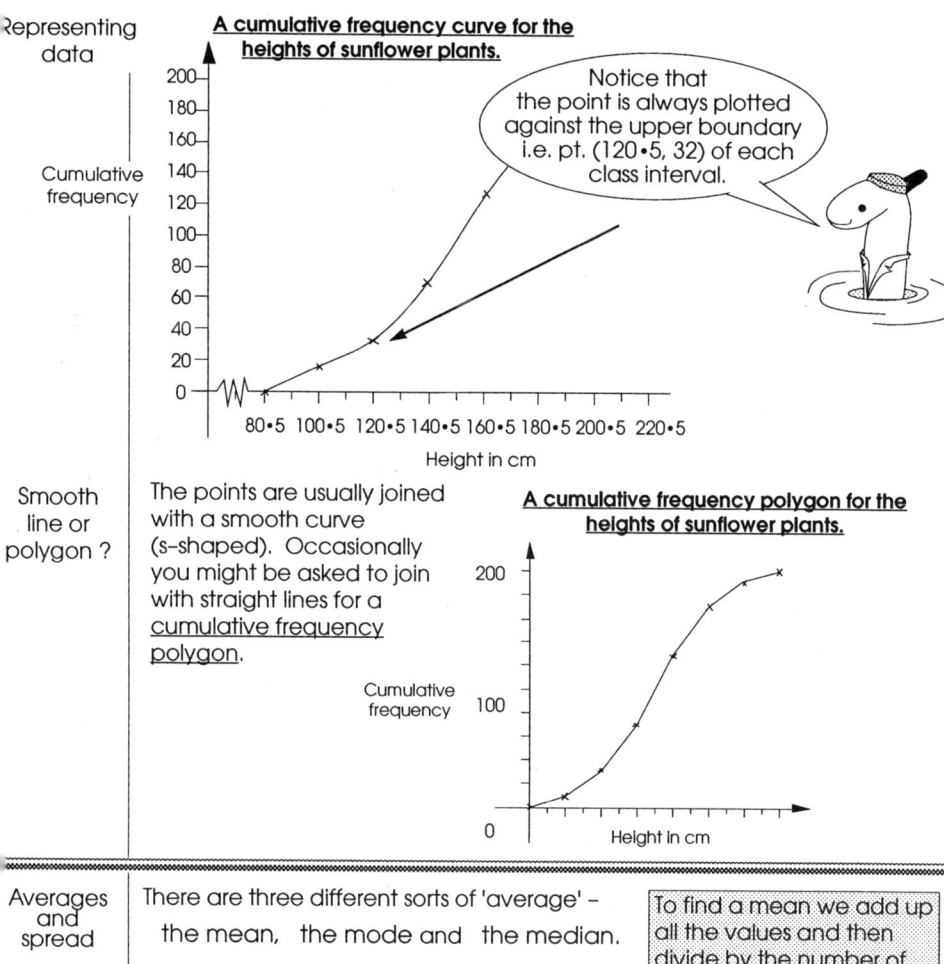

A cumulative frequency curve for the heights of sunflower plants.

Cumulative frequency (y-axis: 0 to 200)
Height in cm (x-axis: 80·5 100·5 120·5 140·5 160·5 180·5 200·5 220·5)

Notice that the point is always plotted against the upper boundary i.e. pt. (120·5, 32) of each class interval.

Smooth line or polygon?

The points are usually joined with a smooth curve (s-shaped). Occasionally you might be asked to join with straight lines for a <u>cumulative frequency polygon</u>.

A cumulative frequency polygon for the heights of sunflower plants.

Cumulative frequency (y-axis: 0, 100, 200)
Height in cm

Averages and spread

Mean

There are three different sorts of 'average' - the mean, the mode and the median.

> To find a mean we add up all the values and then divide by the number of individuals in the sample.

For example we can add up all the children in the country and then divide by the number of families. This will give the mean number of children per family.

If there were 3 pupils; 12 years 2 months, 12 years 4 months, 12 years 9 months. what is their mean age?

①

Mean = 12 yrs 2 m + 12 yrs 4 m + 12 yrs 9 m = $\frac{36 \text{ yrs } 15 \text{ months}}{3}$

⌒ It is easiest here to total the years and months separately ⌒

= 12 yrs 5 months

Mode

> The mode is the value which occurs most often in a set of data.

②

Here is a list of pocket money my friends get each week:-
£5 £2 £3 £2 £3 £4 £2

Three friends get £2. This value occurs the most and so the mode is £2.

| Handling Data | AT 4 |

Median

The median is the middle value when a set of data is organised in order of size.

Find the median value for the pocket money listed above.
Rearrange the list into order of size.

$$2 \quad 2 \quad 2 \quad 3 \quad 3 \quad 4 \quad 5$$

middle value

Median pocket money is £3.

The easiest way to find the mediian is to add 1 to the number of values and divde by 2 $\text{median} = \dfrac{(n+1)}{2}$

If there are an even number of values – find the mean of the middle 2 values.

Range and comparing data

The range is often used when comparing sets of data :
They can have equal means but their ranges may be different.

The range gives an indication of the **spread** of the data.

The previous set of data has a range of £5 – £2 = £3.

Range = Largest value – lowest value

When comparing data give :
the Mean (average)
and the Range

Quartiles

The range can be affected by extreme values (a very high or a very low value)
Once data has been arranged in order of size the median is not the only useful value. One quarter of the way is the lower quartile and three quarters is the upper quartile.

Pocket money: $2 \quad 2 \quad 2 \quad 3 \quad 3 \quad 4 \quad 5$

lower quartile   middle value   upper quartile

Interquartile range = upper quartile – lower quartile
= £4 – £2
= £2

The interquartile range is not affected by extreme values.

Lower quartile range = $\dfrac{(n+1)}{4}$

Upper quartile range = $\dfrac{3(n+1)}{4}$

Averages and spread from frequency distributions

Calculating the mean from a frequency distribution

Mark	Frequency	Mark x Freq.
x	f	fx
4	5	20
5	7	
6	8	
7	8	
8	2	
	30	

> Complete this column yourself.
> Completing the column will help you to find the total number of marks scored.

Mean mark = $\frac{\Sigma fx}{\Sigma f}$ = $\frac{\text{total of (marks} \times \text{frequency)}}{\text{total number of pupils}}$ = $\frac{\quad}{30}$

Σ just means add together. it is pronounced 'sigma'.

= 5.83 marks per pupils (3 s.f.)

Mode

The modal mark is still the mark that occurred most frequently.
8 pupils get 6 marks and 8 pupils got 7 marks so there are 2 modes: 6 and 7.

Median

There are 30 pupils.
The position of the median = $\frac{(n+1)}{2}$
= $\frac{(30+1)}{2}$
= 15.5

The position of the median is halfway between the 15th and 16th mark.

Counting from either end:- the 15th and 16th mark are both in the 6 category so the median mark is 6.

Range

Range can still be calculated:

Range = 8 - 4 = 4
Lower quartile = $\frac{(30+1)}{4}$ = 7.75th mark (the 7th and 8th marks are both 5)
Upper quartile = $\frac{3(30+1)}{4}$ = 23.25th mark (the 23rd and 24th marks are both 7)
Interquartile range = 7 - 5 = 2

Handling Data | **AT 4**

Averages and spread for grouped data

Large quantities of data is often put into convenient groups called classes.

The range of heights reached by beech seedlings in 40 square metres of Hungarian forest measured to the nearest cm.

Grouped frequency distributions

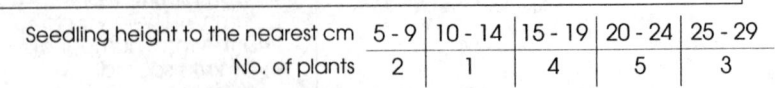

Seedling height to the nearest cm	5 - 9	10 - 14	15 - 19	20 - 24	25 - 29
No. of plants	2	1	4	5	3

A histogram showing the range of heights of beech seedlings.

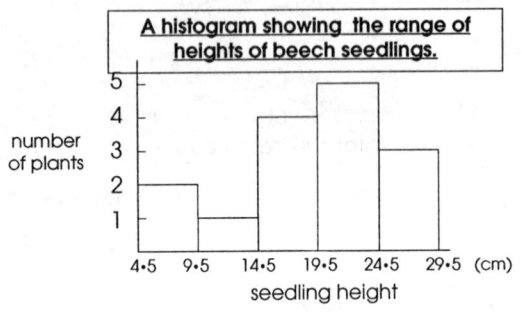

(histogram: number of plants vs seedling height, with x-axis marks at 4·5, 9·5, 14·5, 19·5, 24·5, 29·5 (cm))

Mean

Finding the mean is a bit more difficult.

We pronounce $\bar{x}$ as x bar. $\bar{x}$ stands for the mean and Σ stands for the sum of (or add together).

$$\text{mean} = \bar{x} = \frac{\Sigma fx}{\Sigma f}$$

height	f	x	fx
$4\cdot 5 \leq h < 9\cdot 5$	2	7	14
$9\cdot 5 \leq h < 14\cdot 5$	1	12	12
$14\cdot 5 \leq h < 19\cdot 5$	4	17	68
$19\cdot 5 \leq h < 24\cdot 5$	5	22	110
$24\cdot 5 \leq h < 29\cdot 5$	3	27	81
	Σf 15	Σfx	285

This is the mid-interval value.

$$\text{mean} = \bar{x} = \frac{\Sigma fx}{\Sigma f}$$

$$= \frac{285}{15}$$

$$= 19$$

We are working out an estimate for the mean height.
We do not have the exact values— we assume that all the data in each interval is placed at the mid-interval value.

Modal class

The modal class is the interval which includes the most results. It is the 20 - 24 class in the histogram above.

Median	The median is difficult to calculate from the data- the easiest method is to estimate the median from a cumulative frequency graph. Once the ogive is drawn it can be analysed: **Median** is the middle, or half-way, value or 50th percentile Strictly, the half-way would be at the 100•5th value but when there are lots of values –like here – there is little difference between the 100•5th and the 100th value.
Upper and lower quartiles	The spread or dispersion can be measured. To find the lower quartile :- Find the $\frac{1}{4}$ way value on the cumulative frequency axis (50th value here). Now move horizontally until you meet the ogive. Now move down until you meet the x-axis. These are often given as percentiles. Think of the vertical axis as 0 – 100%. Lower quartile = 25%, upper quartile = 75%.
Inter-quartile range	The interquartile range = upper quartile – lower quartile i.e. in this case it is the range of heights covered by 50% of the sunflower plants. or 75th percentile – 25th percentile

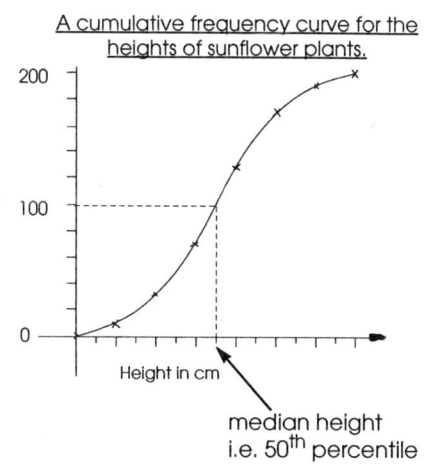

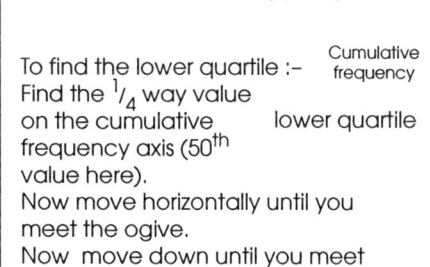

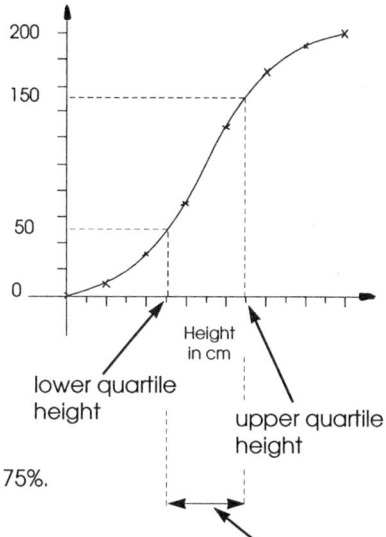

A cumulative frequency curve for the heights of sunflower plants.

median height i.e. 50th percentile

A cumulative frequency curve for the heights of sunflower plants.

lower quartile height

upper quartile height

The interquartile range

Handling Data | **AT 4**

Interpreting data

Once the diagrams are drawn and the averages and measures of spread are calculated, then the data can be interpreted.

Interpret means explain- not just describe. Use the statistics to support your explanations.

Misleading charts

Naughty people can present their figures in a way that is misleading. It is up to us to understand statistics well enough to spot the tricks.

Sales figures

£40 000
£30 000

1991 1992

Sales have not doubled over the year, it just looks like that from the graph because one bar is twice the height of the other.

Beware of charts that don't start at 0. It would have been less misleading to have used broken lines to show this but even better to show the complete graph.

Sales figures

£40 000
£30 000

1991 1992

Flower Sales

Snake's stall   My stall

Although I did sell twice as many flowers as Snake, the figures are misleading because by doubling the length and breadth of the flower, it is now 4 times larger instead of twice as large.

Misleading means

Miss Brown and Mr Jones took the junior pupils on a trip. Two coaches were used. The mean age of all the people on one coach was 12 years 10 months, the mean age on the other coach was 13 years 11 months. Does this mean that all the older children went on one coach?

The mean length of holiday taken abroad by 6 friends is 10 days. One more person is included and the mean length of holiday increases to 16 days. How long a holiday did the latest person take?

How old were the drivers? Where did the teachers sit?

```
7 people  x  16 days  =  112 days
6 people  x  10 days  =   60 days  -
                          52 days
```

The latest person took 52 days holiday. Including this last person has distorted the real picture of the mean length of the holiday. To give some idea of just how distorted, here are the lengths:

   7, 8, 9, 11, 12, 13, 52 days.

Put the values in order of size before you find the middle value.

Median value

The middle value (called the median) would be a better average to represent the group.

Remember, if there is an even number of people, you find the mean of the middle 2 values to find the median.

In this section we are going to show how a result can be affected by the way the data is treated.

We start with the list of breakfast cereals on my left.

Harvest Popo
Golden Crunch Corn
Nature's Wheaties
Amber Rice Crunch
*!~°¬...¥" Chocolate Goodness

I have a theory that most people prefer Harvest Popo (that is my hypothesis).

Some other word that almost tricks you into thinking that this mass produced machine-extruded pretence for a food is not only good for you but was made by a kind country person whose only concern was your continued good health.

Checking the hypothesis

Firstly, collect the data.

Ask a group of 10 people to put the cereals in order of preference (1 = first choice etc).

	A	B	C	D	E	F	G	H	I	J
Harvest Popo	4	3	4	2	1	4	2	3	5	5
Golden Crunch Corn	3	5	2	4	5	5	4	1	4	4
Nature's Wheaties	1	4	3	3	2	3	3	2	2	3
Amber Rice crunch	5	2	1	5	4	2	1	4	1	2
*!~°¬...¥" Chocolate Goodness	2	1	5	1	3	1	5	5	3	1

Interpreting the data

First method

We need to be very careful about sorting this information. There are several different ways to do this but some can give misleading results so be careful.

Cereal	No. of 1st votes
Harvest Popo	1
Golden Crunch Corn	1
Nature's Wheaties	1
Amber Rice crunch	3
*!~°¬...¥" Chocolate Goodness	4

This seems to suggest that *!~°¬...¥" **Chocolate Goodness** is the favourite with $4/10$ 1st choice votes.

Second method

Cereal	No. of 1st votes	No. of 2nd votes	Total
Harvest Popo	1	2	3
Golden Crunch Corn	1	1	2
Nature's Wheaties	1	3	4
Amber Rice crunch	3	3	6
*!~°¬...¥" Chocolate Goodness	4	1	5

We see now, using this method, that **Amber Rice Crunch** is the favourite.

- 101 -

| Handling Data | AT 4 |

Third method
1. Use all the data.
2. Give each choice a score ... 1 for favourite down to 5 for worst.

This gives Harvest Popo: $4 + 3 + 4 + 4 + 2 + 1 + 4 + 2 + 3 + 5 + 5 = 33$

Cereal	Total votes
Harvest Popo	33
Golden Crunch Corn	37
Nature's Wheaties	26
Amber Rice crunch	27
!~¬...¥* Chocolate Goodness	27

We should just check that the total agrees with 10 x 15

5 was the worst and 1 was the best so the lowest total wins.

Analysing results in this way makes **Nature's Wheaties** the favourite breakfast cereal.

So when you interpret statistics you need to be critical about:
> **how the data was collected,**
> **how the diagrams were drawn,**
> **are they correct,**
> **and have appropriate averages been calculated ?**

You need to think about how the enquiry could be improved and suggest further questions for investigation.

Probability

Probability is a measure of chance, It gives an idea of the chance that something will happen or not.

The probability of an event happening can be given as a fraction, a decimal or even as a percentage.
Usually the probability scale is from 0 to 1.
The larger the value of P (the probability) the more likely that the event will occur.

Events which are certain (like death) have a probability of 1 (or 100 %)

An event whose probability is 0 never happens.

```
impossible    unlikely      evens        likely      certain
    |------------|------------|------------|------------|
    0           1/4          1/2          3/4           1
```

e.g. the probability that a fair coin will show tails when tossed is $\frac{1}{2}$ or evens.

Experimental probability	You cannot look at a drawing pin and say what the probability is that it will land point down.

but an experiment could be repeated several times and the results recorded. From these records we can work out the experimental probability.

$$\text{experimental probability} = \frac{\text{number of successful outcomes}}{\text{total number of trials}}$$

trials just means experiments

Long run mean values	I toss this pin 10 times and it lands point upwards 3 times. I toss it 10 more times and it lands point up 4 times. Over these short trials the probability has changed. If I carry on for 200 tosses, I find that it lands point up 83 times.

The probability is $\frac{83}{200} = 41 \cdot 5\%$

you can give the answer as a simple fraction, a decimal fraction or as a percentage.

This is the **long run mean value**. Because the sample is larger, the results tend to be 'firmer' ('firm' being less likely to change)

Theoretical probability	In some situations the possible outcomes (the possible results) are equally likely to happen. Then the probability of an event occurring can be calculated.

$$\text{the probability of an event happening} = \frac{\text{number of successful outcomes}}{\text{total number of possible outcomes}}$$

You could look at an unbiased, six-sided dice and say that the probability of each face coming up is the same.

For example, the probability of tossing a dice and getting a 5 = $\frac{1}{6}$
(There is one 5 and 6 numbers possible)

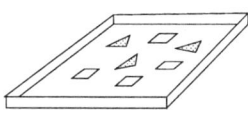

The probability of picking up a square counter is $\frac{4}{7}$ (there are 4 squares and 7 shapes altogether)

Mutually exclusive	When you toss an unbiased dice you can only get the result 1, 2, 3, 4, 5 or 6. If the outcome is 5 – it prevents any other number from happening. These events are called mutually exclusive.

The probabilities of all the possible mutually exclusive events add up to 1.

The possible outcomes from throwing a dice are 1, 2, 3, 4, 5 or 6. The probability of each occurring is $\frac{1}{6}$

Probabilities are $\frac{1}{6} + \frac{1}{6} + \frac{1}{6} + \frac{1}{6} + \frac{1}{6} + \frac{1}{6} = 1$

This is useful and can save time in calculating probabilities.

(continued)

Handling Data — AT 4

Continued from the last page

There are 10 coloured balls in a bag: 3 are red, 4 are black, 2 are white and 1 is blue.

One ball is taken out without looking at it.

Probability it is red = P(red) = $\frac{3}{10}$

Probability it is black = P(black) = $\frac{4}{10}$ = $\frac{2}{5}$

Probability it is white = P(white) = $\frac{2}{10}$ = $\frac{1}{5}$

Probability it is blue = P(blue) = $\frac{1}{10}$

P(green) = 0

The ball could only be red, black, white or blue, so the probabilities must total 1

$\frac{3}{10} + \frac{4}{10} + \frac{2}{10} + \frac{1}{10} = \frac{10}{10} = \frac{1}{1}$

Combined events

We can also work out the probability of combined events e.g. that the ball is either black or white

1

Probability that the ball taken out is black or white
= P(black or white)
= P(black) + P(white)
= $\frac{4}{10} + \frac{2}{10}$
= $\frac{6}{10}$
= $\frac{3}{5}$

2

What is the probability that the ball is <u>not</u> blue?

If the ball is not blue it must be either red, black or white.

There are two ways to calculate this:

so P(not blue) = P(red) + P(black) + P(white)
= $\frac{3}{10} + \frac{4}{10} + \frac{2}{10}$
= $\frac{9}{10}$

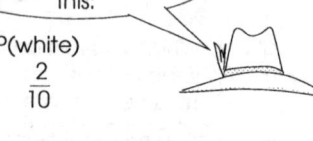

but it is often easier to calculate the probability that the ball is <u>not</u> blue by

P(not blue) = 1 − P(<u>is</u> blue)
= 1 − $\frac{1}{10}$
= $\frac{9}{10}$

This gives an example of the mutually exclusive idea being used.

Relative frequency	Experimental probabilities are used when it is not possible to use theoretical probabilities and sometimes experiments can be performed to test the theoretical probability.

If a dice is fair then we expect the probability of throwing a 4 to be $\frac{1}{6}$

$$P(4) = \frac{1}{6}$$

This is theoretical and not the result of analysing our data.

This doesn't mean that we can expect to get one 4 every six throws.

... but that over a large number of throws you would expect to get $\frac{1}{6}$ of them as 4's.

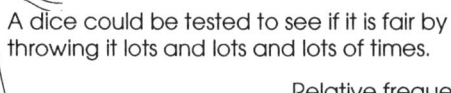

A dice could be tested to see if it is fair by throwing it lots and lots and lots of times.

$$\text{Relative frequency} = \frac{\text{no of times 4 is thrown}}{\text{total number of throws}}$$

As we make more and more throws our confidence in our answer grows.

If, after many throws (like about 500 or more), the answer is close to a sixth then the dice is fair (for throwing a 4).

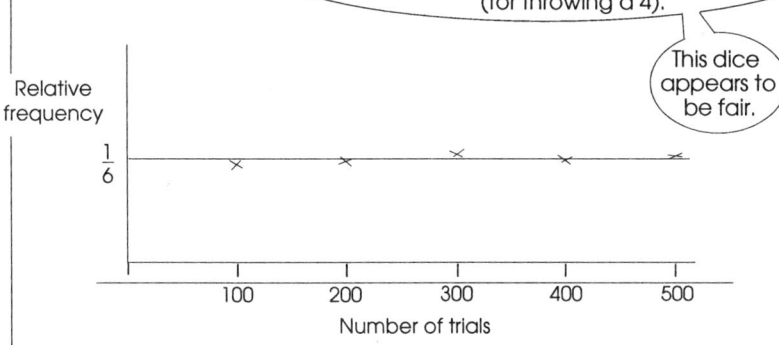

This dice appears to be fair.

Relative frequency vs Number of trials (100, 200, 300, 400, 500) — values plotted at $\frac{1}{6}$.

$$\text{Relative frequency} = \frac{\text{no of times we get a particular result}}{\text{total number of tries}}$$

Independent events	If you roll a dice and then repeat the experiment a second time, the result is not affected by the first roll of the dice.

Independent events are when the outcome of one event does not affect the outcome of another event.

| Handling Data | AT 4 |

Combinations of events

When 2 or more events happen it is useful to set out all the possible results as a diagram.
This could be just a list like the one set out below.

Lists

A coin is tossed twice in succession – the list of possible outcomes is:

(H, H) — First trial could have been a head followed by
(H, T) — another head or a tail.
(T, H) — First trial could have been
(T, T) — a tail followed by a head or another tail.

Probability space diagram

Or instead of list we could have used a probability space diagram.

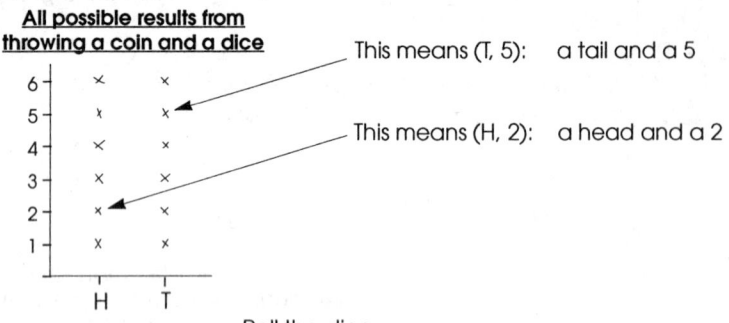

All possible results from throwing a coin and a dice

```
6 -  x    x
5 -  x    x
4 -  x    x
3 -  x    x
2 -  x    x
1 -  x    x
     H    T
```

This means (T, 5): a tail and a 5

This means (H, 2): a head and a 2

Tree diagrams (representing the details shown in the probability space diagram)

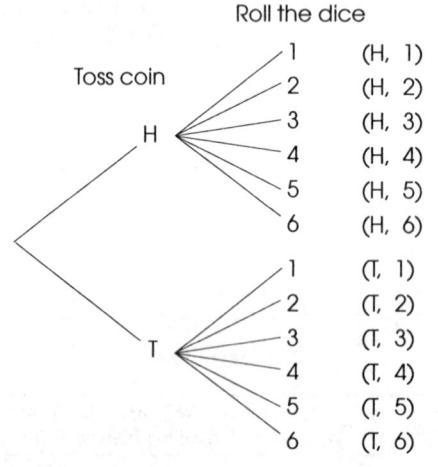

```
              Roll the dice
                   1   (H, 1)
Toss coin          2   (H, 2)
                   3   (H, 3)
         H         4   (H, 4)
                   5   (H, 5)
                   6   (H, 6)
                   1   (T, 1)
                   2   (T, 2)
         T         3   (T, 3)
                   4   (T, 4)
                   5   (T, 5)
                   6   (T, 6)
```

Remember to list all the outcomes (follow the branches)

OR Rule

When 2 mutually exclusive events (A and B) take place, the probability that either A **or** B happens is:

P(A or B) = P(A) + P(B)

When rolling a dice the probability of throwing a 2 or a 5 is:

$$P(2 \text{ or } 5) = P(2) + P(5)$$
$$= \frac{1}{6} + \frac{1}{6} = \frac{2}{6} = \frac{1}{3}$$

AND Rule	When two independent events A and B take place the probability that A **and** B happen is : $$P(A \text{ and } B) = P(A) \times P(B)$$

> The probability of 2 events happening together is less likely than the probability of the events happening on their own so the answer must be smaller.

When rolling a dice and tossing a coin, the probability of getting a 4 and a head is:

$$P(4 \text{ and } H) = P(4) \times P(H)$$
$$= \frac{1}{6} \times \frac{1}{2} = \frac{1}{12}$$

Here are some examples using diagrams and combined probabilities:

Combination of events

> This table shows all the possible results when a coin is tossed **and** a counter is chosen from 4 coloured counters.

> These are the full 8 events because whenever one outcome happens it prevents another happening.

	blue	red	green	yellow
Heads	HB	HR	HG	HY
Tails	TB	TR	TG	TY

What is the probability of getting 1 result out of 8 possible results if they are equally likely to happen,

Answer $\frac{1}{8}$ or 0.125

N.B. The total sum of events is 1

Probability of choosing a red <u>and</u> a head at the same time:

$$P(\text{red} \underline{\text{ and }} \text{head}) = P(\text{red}) \times P(\text{head})$$
$$= \frac{1}{4} \times \frac{1}{2} = \frac{1}{8}$$

N.B. The probability of getting a <u>red</u> and a <u>head</u> is less likely than the probability of getting a red by itself ($^1/_4$)

or a head by itself ($^1/_2$)

- 107 -

| Handling Data | AT 4 |

Tree diagrams

The probability that it will rain on any day at the sea side is $\frac{1}{10}$

Snake is going there on holiday for 2 days and wants to know how likely it is that she will get only one wet day.

We can work out the answer for her by using a tree diagram.

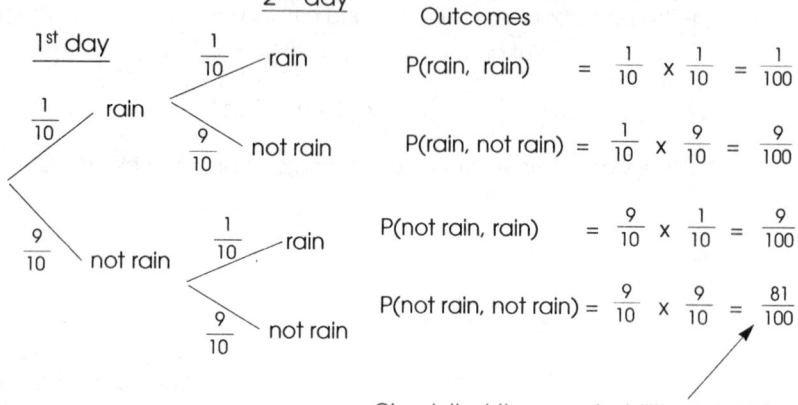

```
                    2nd day
    1st day                              Outcomes
              1/10 — rain      P(rain, rain)     = 1/10 × 1/10 = 1/100
         rain
    1/10
              9/10 — not rain  P(rain, not rain) = 1/10 × 9/10 = 9/100
    
              1/10 — rain      P(not rain, rain) = 9/10 × 1/10 = 9/100
    9/10
         not rain
              9/10 — not rain  P(not rain, not rain) = 9/10 × 9/10 = 81/100
```

Check that these probabilities total 1

$$\frac{1}{100} + \frac{9}{100} + \frac{9}{100} + \frac{81}{100} = 1$$

Follow the branches to get all the outcomes – following one branch and then another means you multiply the probabilities.

The wet day could be either wet on day 1 or wet on day 2.
Outcomes needed:

$$P(\text{rain, not rain}) = \frac{1}{10} \times \frac{9}{10} = \frac{9}{100}$$

$$P(\text{not rain, rain}) = \frac{9}{10} \times \frac{1}{10} = \frac{9}{100}$$

So
P(rain on one day) = P(rain, not rain) **or** P(not rain, rain)

$$= \frac{9}{100} + \frac{9}{100}$$

$$= \frac{18}{100} = \frac{9}{50}$$

or 18%

For your notes.

Introduction

Here are some questions on those topics where people are known to make the most mistakes.

We have put the answers at the end of the guide. There is then less of a temptation to look at them before you have a try at the answer for yourself. Don't feel guilty if you do look though (just try not to look next time).

If you get hopelessly lost when doing one of these questions, and if the answers don't help, have a look in the text to see whether there is a worked example there to help you. In short: keep plugging away until you find a way through, doing this will help you in the exams.

Hints for scoring higher marks

Don't use correcting fluid,

Cross out wrong working so that it can still be read, just put a line through it. (It may still be correct). **(Never cross out until the second answer has been completed)**.

Put one answer only in the answer space. Putting in 2 answers gets no marks.

Make sure that your calculator is in degree mode.

Remember that when writing amounts of money we must put ,2 digits in the pence column: 3•6 on the calculator ⟹ £3•60 in the answer.

Examination practice paper.

1. 21% of £49•00 is approximately £10•00.
   a. Write down the calculation using estimated values in order to arrive at this answer.
   b. Calculate the correct value of 21% of £49•00 .

2. 'If you add an odd and an even number together you get an odd number'.
   a. Give 2 examples to show that this is always true.
   b. Let one even number be 2K and (2K − 1) be the number before it. Show that the sum of them must be an odd number i.e. prove that the statement at the beginning of the question is true.

3. Solve the equation:

   a. i. $y - 7 = 4$　　　　iii. $4 - 2z = 3 + 5z$
      ii. $\frac{1}{2}x + 4 = 3$

   b. Simplify:　i. $4(b + 4) - 2(b - 2)$
      　　　　　ii. $(a + b + c) - (a - b - c)$

   c. In a garden there are x pansies. There are twice as many roses as pansies. There are also 36 delphiniums.
      i. The total of all of these flowers is 102.
         Write down an equation in x and solve it.
      ii. How many roses are there?

   d. i. Fill in the next 2 terms in the the following sequence:
         x, 2x, 3x, 5x, 8x, —, —,
      ii. Explain how you got your answer.

4. A rectangular meadow is 16 m wide and 33 m long. At one corner a goat is tethered on a chain 14m long. A cow grazes the rest of the meadow.
   a. Using a scale of 2cm to 10m, draw a plan of the meadow.
   b. Draw the locus of the region in which the goat can graze.
   c. Find the area of the region the goat grazes correct to 3 sig. figs.
   d. Find the area that the cow grazes correct to 3 significant figures.
   e. Write down the ratio of the area the goat grazes to the area the cow grazes in its lowest terms.

5. Six chickens are kept in a controlled environment. The number of eggs laid by the six was recorded for 200 days. The bar chart on the right displays the results.

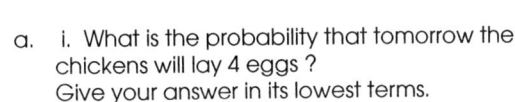

   a. i. What is the probability that tomorrow the chickens will lay 4 eggs?
         Give your answer in its lowest terms.
      ii. Why might your answer not be sensible?

   b. 3 of the chickens lay brown eggs and 3 of the chickens lay large eggs. If you get 6 eggs one day, explain why you cannot calculate the probability of at least one of the eggs being a large brown.

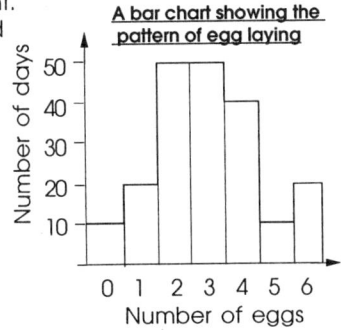

A bar chart showing the pattern of egg laying

Questions

6. An average cherry cake for 6 people uses the following ingredients:
   3 eggs,
   4 oz sugar,
   4 oz flour,
   1 teaspoon yeast,
   116 cherries.
   Bill wants to make the cake for 8 people.

   a. Adapt this recipe for the 8 people (rounding off your answers sensibly).

   b. The recipe says bake at 425 °F. By using the following formula convert this to degrees Celsius.
   $$C = \frac{5}{9}(F - 32).$$
   Round off your answer to the nearest 10°.

7. Express, in terms of n, the next term in these sequences:

   a. $\frac{0}{1}, \frac{1}{2}, \frac{2}{3}, \frac{3}{4},$

   b. $(-1)^2, (-2)^3, (-3)^4, (-4)^5,$

   c. Find the sum of the first 3 terms of the sequence n^2.

   d. 3 bananas and 5 pears cost £1·10
   6 bananas and 1 pear cost £1·30
   If the cost of a banana is b pence and the cost of a pear is p pence, write down 2 equations connecting b and p and solve them to find b and p.

8. The volume of this cube is 6·5 cm³.
   a. By the method of trial and improvement, find the length of one side.

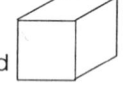

   b. What is an approximate degree of accuracy? Explain why.

9. Jan cycles to school. She always times herself.
   These are the result of 21 journeys.

Time (mins)	8	9	10	11	12
Number of journeys	1	4	5	7	4

   a. Work out the range of her times,

   b. Work out the mean journey time. Give your answer correct to 1 d.p.

   c. What is the modal time?

   d. What is the median time?

10. The distance to a holiday resort airport in Cyprus is 2310 miles.
    20 years ago an aircraft took 4 hrs. 10 mins. to fly there.

    a. Calculate the average speed. Give your answer in standard form.

    b. The flying time was later reduced by 16 mins. What is the percentage change in the speed.

    c. Light travels at a speed of $1 \cdot 86 \times 10^5$ miles/s.
       Calculate how many seconds it would take you to get to Cyprus if you could travel at the speed of light.

11.

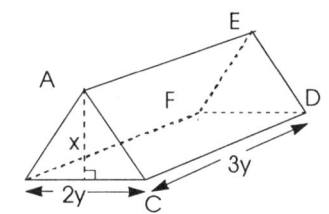

△ ABC = △ EFD
Both are equilateral triangles.
x is the perpendicular height of △ ABC

   a. What is the name of the solid ABCDEF ?

   b. Write down the sum of the lengths of all the edges.

   c. Write down an expression for the area of ABC and simplify it.

   d. Write down an expression for the volume of the solid.

   e. By considering △ ABC find an equation connecting x and y.

12. a. Solve the inequality $4x - 6 \geq 4$

    b. If x is a whole number where $-2 \leq x \leq 3$.
       Find the numbers which satisfy this inequality $4x \leq 2x + 3$

    c. The height a golf ball reaches when hit is given by the formula $s = ut - 5t^2$.
       u is the speed that it leaves the club at, in m/s.
       t is the time since it was hit.

       i. Find s after 3 seconds if it leaves the club at 20m/s.
       ii. The ball hits the ground when the height = 0.
           Find how many seconds the ball is in flight before the height = 0.

13. Solve the value of a and b from these simultaneous equations.

$$7a + 6b = 7 \quad ①$$
$$8a = 3(1 - 3b) \quad ②$$

Questions

14.
a. 0·394 inches = 1cm
Calculate how many centimetres = 1 inch to 3 sig. figs.

b. Draw a square of side 1 inch. What is its area in cm^2 ?

c. Given that 2·2 lb = 1 kg.
Change 30 lbs to kg correct 2 sig. fig.

d. Old tyre pressure gauges are calibrated in both imperial and metric measurements.
Use your corrected answers to convert 30 lbs per square inch to kg per cm^2. (In this case the question asks you to use corrected answers so it is OK to do so, normally we wouldn't.)

15. The probability of having a boy is 0·509.

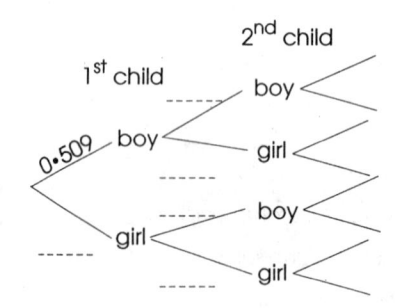

a. If 1000 babies were born how many girls would you expect ?

b. Complete the tree diagram for a family of 3 children filling in the blanks and finishing the branches.

c. What is the probability that the first 2 children are boys.

d. What is the probability that the family of 3 children is not all girls.

16. Pink grapefruits cost 27 pence each. You have £5·00:

a. Without using a calculator, calculate how many you can buy and what change you get. Show all your workings clearly.

b. You can buy a box of 20 grapefruit for £5·00. What percentage price reduction is this ?

17. Convert non-decimal values to decimals
List all values in descending order :

    0·36   36·4% $\frac{1}{3}$ 0·294 $\frac{13}{36}$ 30%

18. a. Multiply the brackets and simplify your results.
    i. $(2x - 4)(x - 7)$
    ii. $(p - q)(q + p)$

   b. Rearrange and make x the subject of these formulae.
    i. $ax + by = z$
    ii. $\dfrac{x + y}{7} = z$

   c. $z = \dfrac{\pi}{4}(1 + \sqrt{Q})$
    i. calculate z if $Q = 1\cdot 21$
    ii. Calculate Q if $z = 200$. Give your answers correct to 3 sig. figs.

19. Joe cycles every day for a week.
    Each day he rounds off his journey to the nearest kilometre.
    These were his distances :
        29 km, 15 km, 43 km, 27 km, 25 km, 20 km, 9 km,
    a. What is the shortest total distance he could have covered ?
    b. What is the largest total distance possible ?
    c. What is the largest possible mean average of a days cycle ride ?

20. The height of a plant is $(3x + 2)$ cm. Another plant is $(2x + 14)$ cm high. The second plant is twice the height of the first plant.
    a. Write down an equation connecting the heights of the two plants.
    b. Solve the equation to find x and hence the height of the 2 plants.

21. a. Factorise:
    i. $ab + ax$
    ii. $2x^2 + 4x$
   b. Simplify:
    i. $(x + 2)(x - 3)$
    ii. $y^2 + 2y + 5y + 5y^2$

22. You want to do a survey on the opinions of people on the welfare of animals.
    a. Write a biased question about caged birds.
    b. Name one place you would get a group of people who thought animal welfare was important.
    c. Explain why there may be no correlation between money spent per household on animal care and the number of animals kept.

Questions

23. Chick-Grow are trying to breed a new type of chicken. The table shows details from a random selection of the flock.

Weight	Mid-point	Frequency	Cumulative Frequency
1 kg up to 2 kg		12	
2 kg up to 3 kg		23	
3 kg up to 4 kg		37	
4 kg up to 5 kg		28	

   a. Complete the mid-point column.
   b. Complete the cumulative frequency column.
   c. Draw a cumulative frequency graph and hence find the median weight.
   d. Find the upper and lower quartile and hence the interquartile range.
   e. Complete an extra column in an appropriate way to calculate the mean weight.

24. A man is 2m tall. He stands on a cliff which is 30m high. A ship is 1.2km out to sea.

   Calculate the angle of depression of the ship from the man.

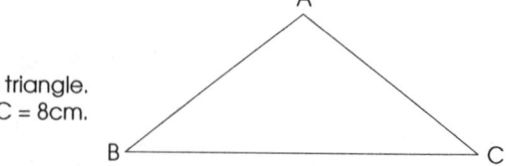

25. ABC is an isoscleles triangle.
   AB = AC = 5cm. BC = 8cm.
   Find angles:

   a. $\hat{ABC}$
   b. $\hat{BCA}$
   c. $\hat{BAC}$

26. △ ABC has coordinates A = (0, 1) B = (-1, 3) C = (-1, 1)
   △ A'B'C' has coordinates A' = (-1, 0) B' = (-3, 1) C' = (-1, 1)
   △ A"B"C" has coordinates A" = (3, 1) B" = (2, 3) C" = (2, 1)
   Draw these of graph paper.
   You will need 4 quadrants and remember to label the x and y axes.

   a. What transformation maps △ ABC → △ A'B'C' ?
   b. What transformation maps △ ABC → △ A"B"C" ?
   c. Reflect △ A'B'C' in the line y = x. Label it △ PQR
   d. What single transformation maps △ ABC → △ PQR ?

27. Plot the graphs of $y = x^2 + 2$ and $y = 3 - x$ for $-2 \leq x \leq 2$
    Solve the equation $x^2 + 2 = 3 - x$

28. a. Factorise $x^2 - 2x - 3$
    b. Solve the equation
       $x^2 - 2x - 3 = 0$

Answers

1. a. $\frac{20}{100} \times 50$ or $0{\cdot}2 \times 50$

   b. $0{\cdot}21 \times 49 = £10{\cdot}29$

2. a. $2 + 3 = 5$ etc.
   b. $2K + (2K - 1) = 4K - 1$ $4K$ is even so $4K - 1$ is odd.

3. a. i. $y = 11$
      ii. $x = -2$
      iii. $\frac{1}{7}$

   b. i. $2b + 20$
      ii. $2b + 2c$

   c. i. $3x + 36 = 102 \Rightarrow x = 22$
      ii. $2 \times 22 = 44$ roses

   d. i. $13x, 21x$
      ii. Add the two previous terms.

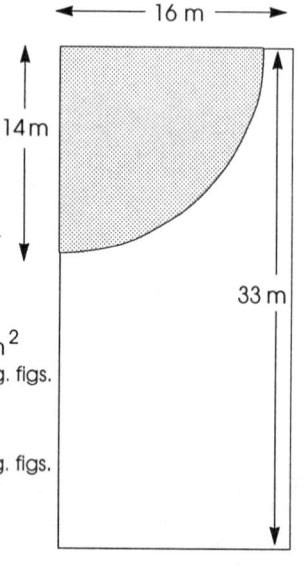

4. a. ⎫
   b. ⎬ ─────────────→
   c. Area $= \pi r^2 \div 4$
      $= (\pi \times 14^2) \div 4 = 153{\cdot}86 = 154\,m^2$
      correct to 3 sig. figs.
   d. Area the cow eats $= (16 \times 33) - 153{\cdot}86$
      $= 374\,m^2$
      correct to 3 sig. figs.
   e. $154 : 374$ (Both have a factor of 22)
      $7 : 17$

   (Diagram: 16 m wide, 14 m and 33 m heights, with shaded quarter-circle region.)

5. a. i. $\frac{40}{200} = \frac{1}{5}$ this is using relative frequency.

      ii. Chickens are living creatures. They grow older or may get ill.

   b. Because being large or being brown are not mutually exclusive. An egg could be both large and brown or could be brown and small, or white and large.

6. a. $3 \times \frac{8}{6} = 4$ eggs $\qquad 4 \times \frac{8}{6} = 5\dot{\cdot}3$
   $\qquad\qquad\qquad\qquad\qquad\qquad\quad = 5\frac{1}{3}$ oz flour and sugar (or $5\frac{1}{2}$)
   $1 \times \frac{8}{6} = 1\dot{\cdot}3$
   $\qquad\quad = 1\frac{1}{3}$ tsp yeast and
   $116 \times \frac{8}{6} = 154\dot{\cdot}6$ or 155 cherries

   b. $C = \frac{5}{9}(425 - 32)$ (use brackets or do that piece last)
   $\quad = 218\dot{\cdot}3 \approx 220°C$

7. a. $\frac{n-1}{n}$

   b. $(-n)^{n+1}$

   c. $1^2 + 2^2 + 3^2 = 1 + 4 + 9 = 14$

   d. $3b + 5p = 110$
      $6b + p = 130 \qquad b = 20 \quad p = 10$

8. a. The length must lie between 1 and 2 because $1^3 = 1$ and $2^3 = 8$
   So 1·8 or 1·9 is a suitable starting point.
   $\qquad\qquad 1\cdot8^3 = 5\cdot83$ too small
   $\qquad\qquad 1\cdot9^3 = 6\cdot86$ too large
   $\qquad\qquad$ The answer = 1·9

   b. You would measure a cube to the nearest mm so 1 decimal place is an appropriate degree of accuracy so $1\cdot9^3$ gives the answer nearest to $6\cdot5cm^3$

9. a. $12 - 8 = 4$ (you must do the subtraction to get a single answer)

   b. $\frac{(8 \times 1) + (9 \times 4) + (10 \times 5) + (11 \times 7) + (12 \times 4)}{21}$

   $\frac{8 + 36 + 50 + 77 + 48}{21}$

   $= 10\cdot4$

   c. 11 mins (you have 7 of these)

   d. 11 mins ($\frac{21 + 1}{2} = 11^{th}$ the value needed)
   $\qquad\qquad\qquad\qquad 11^{th}$ value, in order, is in the 11 min category.

Answers

10. a. speed $= \dfrac{\text{distance}}{\text{time}}$

    speed $= \dfrac{2310}{4\,{}^{10}/_{60}}$ (use a $^b/_c$ or calculate as a decimal and put in the memory)

    $= 554\,\tfrac{2}{5}$ mph

    $= 554.4$ mph

    $= 5.544 \times 10^2$ mph

  b. New time $= 3$ hrs 54 mins
     New speed $= 592.30769$ mph   (don't round off yet)

     % increase $= \dfrac{592.30769 - 554.4}{554.4} \times 100$

     $= 6.84\%$ correct to 2 decimal places

  c. $t = \dfrac{d}{s} \Rightarrow t = \dfrac{2.31 \times 10^3}{(1.86 \times 10^5)} = 1.24 \times 10^{-2}$ secs

  (use the EXP button and use Min or store)

11. a. Triangular prism

  b. $(2y + 2y + 2y) \times 2 + 3y \times 3$ (don't forget the brackets)
     $= 12y + 9y$
     $= 21y$

  c. Area $= \dfrac{1}{2} \times 2y \times x$ ($\tfrac{1}{2} \times$ base $\times$ height)
     $= xy$ (simplify)

  d. Vol $= xy \times 3y$ (area of uniform cross section x length)
     $= 3xy^2$ (again simplify)

  e. $x^2 + y^2 = (2y)^2$ using Pythagoras' theorem
                        $(2y \times 2y = 4y^2)$
     $\Rightarrow x^2 + y^2 = 4y^2$
           $x^2 = 3y^2$ (this line would get you full marks)
           $x = \sqrt{3}\,y$

12. a. $x \geq 2.5$

    b. $-2, -1, 0, 1$

    c. i. 15m
        ii. $0 = 20t - 5t^2$
            $\Rightarrow 0 = 4t - t^2$ so $t = 0$ or 4 secs
            $0 = t(4-t)$ i.e. time = 4 seconds
            so $t = 0$ or 4 seconds   (the ball is on the ground when $t = 0$)

13. First multiply the brackets out and rearrange to match ① .

    $7a + 6b = 7$ ① × 8
    $8a + 9b = 3$ ② × 7
    $\Rightarrow 56a + 48b = 56$
    $56a + 63b = 21$ subtract
    $-15b = 35$
    $b = -2\frac{1}{3}$ or $2.\dot{3}$ Don't round off the answers.
    $a = 3$

14. a. $\frac{1}{0.394} = 2.54$ cm

    b. Area = 6.5 cm^2
        (or 6.45 cm^2 to 3 sig. fig.)

    c. $\frac{30}{2.2}$ kg = 13.63 = 14   (to 2 sig. fig.)

    d. $\frac{14}{6.5} = 2.2$ kg per cm^2

15. a. $1 - 0.509 = 0.491$ 491 girls

    b. All boys are 0.509 all girl branches = 0.491

    c. $0.509 \times 0.509 = 0.259081$

    d. P(all girls) = 0.491^3
              = 0.1183707
        P(no girls) = $1 -$ P(all girls)
              = 0.8816291
              ≈ 0.88

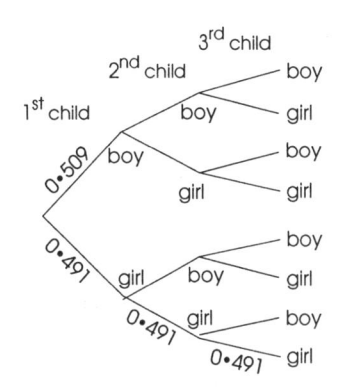

- 121 -

Answers

16. a.
```
      18
  27 ) 500
      27
      ---
      230
      216
      ---
       14
```
Buy 18 with 14p change.

b. Now cost 25p each

$$\text{deduction} = \frac{(27 - 25)}{27} \times 100 = 7.4\%$$

17. 0.36   36.4% $\frac{1}{3}$ 0.294 $\frac{13}{36}$ 30%

0.364,   0.361,   0.36,   0.3̇,   0.3,   0.294.

18. a. i. $2x^2 - 18x + 28$

ii. $pq + p^2 - q^2 - pq = p^2 - q^2$

b. i. $x = \frac{z - by}{a}$ or $x = \frac{z}{a} - \frac{by}{a}$

ii. $x = 7z - y$

c. i. $z = 1.65$

ii. $200 = \frac{\pi}{4}(1 + \sqrt{Q})$ Substitute and **then** rearrange

$\Rightarrow \frac{800}{\pi} - 1 = \sqrt{Q} \Rightarrow Q = 64300$

19. a. $28.5 + 14.5 + 42.5 + 26.5 + 24.5 + 19.5 + 8.5 = 164.5$ km

b. 171.5

c. 24.5 km (which rounds up to 25 km)

20. a. $2(3x + 2) = (2x + 14)$

b. $6x + 4 = 2x + 14$
$4x = 10$
$x = 2.5$ cm

$3x + 2 = 3 \times 2.5 + 2 = 9.5$ cm   and   19 cm

21. a. i.   a(b + x)
    ii. 2x(x + 2)

    b. i. $x^2 - x - 6$
    ii. $6y^2 + 7y = y(6y + 7)$

22. There are many possible accurate answers for this type of question – The following are some suggestions:
    a. Don't you think it is cruel to shut birds up in cages?
    b. In the vets waiting room. (At a protest march for animal rights).
    c. Size of animal e.g. alsation dogs or caged hamsters.

23.

Mid-point	Frequency	C. F.	midpoint x freq
1·5	12	12	1·5 x 12 = 18
2·5	23	35	57·5
3·5	37	72	129·5
4·5	28	100	126
		Total	331

    a.   b.   e.

    c. Median value   3·45 kg   (any value from 3·4 – 3·5 is acceptable)

    d. L.Q = 2·65 kg   U.Q. = 4·15 kg
       I.Q.R. = 4·15 – 2·65 = 1·5 kg   (1·4 – 1·6 is acceptable)

    e. 331 ÷ 100 = 3·31 kg

24. $\alpha = \tan^{-1} \frac{32}{1200} = 15\cdot 3°$ (to 3 sig. fig.)

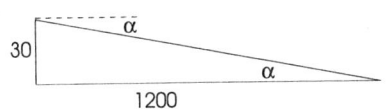

    The diagram is not to scale

25. a. $\widehat{ABC} = \cos^{-1}\frac{4}{5} = 36\cdot 9°$
    b. $\widehat{BCA} = 36\cdot 9°$
    c. 106·2°

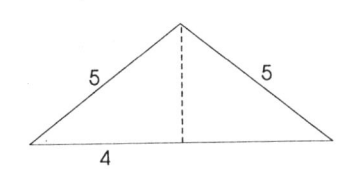

Answers

26. a. Reflection in the line y = -x
   or   x + y = 0

   b. Translation through $\begin{bmatrix} 3 \\ 0 \end{bmatrix}$

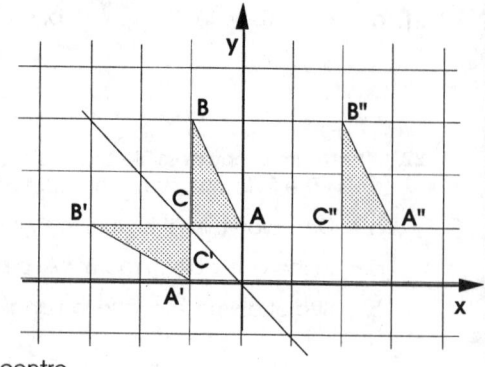

   d. Rotation of 180° or $\frac{1}{2}$ turn, centre of rotation (0, 0) or origen.

27.

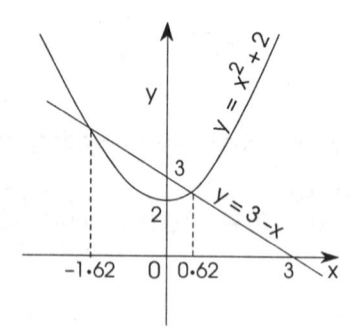

x = 0.62   or   x = -1.62

28. a. (x - 3)(x + 1)

   b. x = 3 or -1

Index

Acute angle, 57
Addition (negatives), 5
Algebra, 30
Algebraic manipulation, 38
And rule, 107
Angles, 57, 58, 59
Approximations, 7, 8, 28
Arc, 63
Area, 64, 86, 70, 71
Average rates, 24
Averages, 95
Bar charts, 90
Bar graphs, 90
Bar-line graphs, 91
Bearings, 60
Bisector of an angle, 68
Brackets, 40
Calendar, 27
Cardinal numbers, 2
Chord, 63
Circles, 63
Circumference, 63
Co-ordinates, 42
Collecting data, 89
Combined events, 104, 106, 107
Common difference, 30
Commutative operations, 3
Compound interest, 18
Compound measure, 26
Congruent shapes, 62
Constructions, 67
Continuous data, 88
Conversion graphs, 47
Conversions, 69
Converting units, 25
Correlation, 93
Cube roots, 11
Cubic (graph), 46
Cumulative frequency, 94
Dash notation, 21
Data, 88, 89
Decimal places, 7
Decimals, 2
Descartes, 42
Diameter, 63
Direct proportion, 22
Discrete data, 88
Distributions, 90
Division, 5, 6
Enlargement, 73, 74, 75
Equations, 32
Equilateral triangle, 61
Equivalent fractions, 14
Estimating, 55
Even numbers, 9
Exchange rates, 23
Experimental probability, 103
Exponential decay, 29
Exterior angles, 58
Factorising, 40, 41
Factors, 9
Flow charts, 34
Formula, 32, 33, 35, 37, 85

Fractions, 13, 15, 16, 22
Fractions (adding), 39
Frequency diagrams, 92
Frequency polygons, 92
Gradients, 48
Graphs, 42
Graphs (basic shapes), 45
Grids, 73
Grouped data, 98
Grouped frequency distribution, 92
Highest common factor, 10
Hypothesis, 90
Imperial measure, 68
Imperial units, 25
Independent events, 105
Index notation, 12
Indices, 12
Indices (simplifying), 39
Inequalities, 50, 51
Integers, 2
Interest, 18
Interior angles, 58
Interpretation, 102
Interpreting data, 100
Interquartile range, 100
Inverse correlation, 93
Inverse proportion, 22
Isosceles triangle, 6, 84
Kite, 61
LCM, 10
Like terms, 38
Line graphs, 91
Line of best fit, 93
Linear, 45, 49
Linear measurements, 55
Lists, 106
Loci, 66
Long run median values, 103
Lowest common multiple, 10
Mean, 98, 99
Median, 96, 97
Metric measure, 68
Metric measurement, 25
Mirror, 76
Misleading charts, 100
Misleading data, 100
Mixed units, 26
Modal class, 98
Mode, 95, 97
Multiples, 9
Multiplication (negatives), 5
Mutually exclusive, 103
Negative numbers, 5
Net, 54
Obtuse angle, 57
Odd numbers, 9
Ogive, 94
One-way stretches, 81
Operations, 3
OR rule, 106
Ordering numbers, 14
Parallel, 60
Parallelogram, 61

Index

Percentages, 16, 17, 18
Perimeters, 55
Perpendicular bisector, 67
Pictograms, 90
Pie chart, 19, 91
Place value, 2
Plane, 60
Plotting positions, 60
Powers, 12
Prime numbers, 9
Probability, 102
Probability space diagram, 106
Properties of numbers, 9
Proportion, 20
Proportionality, 49, 50
Pure numbers, 6
Pyramids, 55
Pythagoras, 69, 70
Quadratic, 31
Quadratic (graph), 45
Qualitative, 88
Quantitative, 88
Quartiles, 96, 99
Radius, 63
Range, 96, 97
Rates, 23
Rates of change, 47
Ratio, 20, 21
Recipes, 22
Reciprocal, 13, 34
Reciprocal (graph), 45
Rectangle, 61
Reduction, 73, 74, 75
Reflections, 76, 77
Reflex angle, 57
Regions, 52
Relative frequency, 105
Representing data, 95
Rhombus, 61
Right angle, 57
Roots, 11
Rotations, 77, 78
Rounding, 6, 8

Rounding remainders, 7
Scale drawings, 56
Scale factors, 80
Scales, 60, 68
sequences, 30
Significant figures, 7
Similar shapes, 62
Sketching, 54
Solids (& nets), 54
Solving equations, 35, 36, 41, 43
Spread, 95
Square, 61
Square roots, 11
Squares, 11
Squares (difference of two), 40
Squaring brackets, 40
Standard index form, 13
Statistics, 88 et seq.
Straight angle, 57
Subtend, 65
Subtraction (negatives), 5
Symmetries, 75, 76, 77
Tangent, 63
Tesselations, 62
Three dimensional objects, 54
Time, 27
Transformations, 78
Translations, 79
Trapezium, 61
Travel graph, 46
Tree diagrams, 108
Trial and improvement, 37
Triangle, 61
Trigonometry, 83
Two way tables, 19
Unitary form, 20
Units, 25
Variables, 30
VAT, 18
Vectors, 79
Vertically opposite angle, 57
Volume, 72